Textuality and the Bible

Textuality and the Bible

Michael B. Shepherd

WIPF & STOCK · Eugene, Oregon

TEXTUALITY AND THE BIBLE

Copyright © 2016 Michael B. Shepherd. All rights reserved. Except for brief quotations in critical publications or reviews, no part of this book may be reproduced in any manner without prior written permission from the publisher. Write: Permissions, Wipf and Stock Publishers, 199 W. 8th Ave., Suite 3, Eugene, OR 97401.

Wipf & Stock
An Imprint of Wipf and Stock Publishers
199 W. 8th Ave., Suite 3
Eugene, OR 97401

www.wipfandstock.com

PAPERBACK ISBN: 978-1-4982-8277-2
HARDCOVER ISBN: 978-1-4982-8279-6

Manufactured in the U.S.A.

For Ava

Contents

Introduction | ix

1 Orality and Textuality | 1
2 Self-aware Bookishness | 10
3 Canon Consciousness | 26
4 Torah lishma | 38
5 A Study in Variant Literary Editions | 61
6 A Grammatical Study | 78
7 A Study in Semantics | 94

Bibliography | 103

Introduction

EACH NEW GENERATION OF the people of God must grapple with the reality that God has revealed himself in a book. It must ask what the significance of that reality is for the life of faith.[1] History shows that renewed interest in the reading and interpretation of the text of Scripture has punctuated all the major periods in the community of believers.[2] At the end of Moses' life he explained the Torah to the people (Deut 1:5). He also wrote the Torah and gave instructions to read the Torah publicly on a regular basis after his death (Deut 31:9–13). The impetus and basis for Josiah's religious reforms was the discovery of the "book" (*sefer*) of the Torah and the subsequent public reading of it (2 Kgs 22–23).[3] Reestablishment of the post-exilic community took place under the leadership of Ezra (Ezra 7:6, 10) who read and expounded the book of the Torah in accordance with Moses' original instructions (Neh 8–9). The NT authors repeatedly acknowledged the critical role

---

1. " . . . the biblical texts must be investigated for their own sake to the extent that the revelation which they attest does not stand or occur, and is not to be sought, behind or above them but in them. If in reply it is asked whether Christianity is really a book-religion, the answer is that strangely enough Christianity has always been and only been a living religion when it is not ashamed to be actually and seriously a book-religion" (Barth, *Church Dogmatics*, 494–95).

2. See Fishbane, *Biblical Interpretation*, 32–37.

3. The Hebrew term *sefer* does not refer in this context to a "book" in the sense of a codex or a bound document. The translation "book" is appropriate where *sefer* refers to a large literary work as opposed to a smaller document such as a letter. See Schniedewind, *How the Bible Became a Book*, 4.

Introduction

of the Hebrew Scriptures in their understanding of the life, death, and resurrection of Christ (e.g., Luke 24:25-27, 44-47; John 1:45; 5:46; Rom 1:2; 3:21-22; 16:25-26; 2 Tim 3:15-16). The Protestant Reformation had its beginnings in a return prompted by the Renaissance to the written sources (*ad fontes*) of the faith.[4] Martin Luther's German translation of the Bible and John Calvin's commentaries were the pillars of that era.

Of course, large swaths of that same history were plagued by long droughts (Isa 29:9-12; Amos 8:11-14; Dan 12:4). The defining moments mentioned above were offset by movements that deemphasized the Bible either in theory or in practice. Biblical illiteracy in modern churches is well documented, and the decline of biblical language courses in the education of leaders is not helping the situation. Even those who favor in principle an expository approach to teaching the Bible often appear to have little idea of what is involved in the execution of such an approach. That the Bible is a text (or a text made of texts) is not news to anyone, but in actual practice the object of study in what usually passes for biblical interpretation is often far from clear. So-called introductions to the Bible typically spend more time introducing the ancient world of the Bible than they do introducing the literature itself. Sermons are at best reenactments of biblical events, attempts to isolate life principles, or proof-texting in the service of orthodox dogma. At worst they are exercises in pop psychology/philosophy and motivational speaking. Theologies of the Bible frequently bypass the form and sequence of the Bible in favor of some other arrangement.[5] It is not difficult to trace the correlation between this virtual

---

4. "Through the rediscovery of the writings of antiquity and their wide distribution enabled by printing, the humanists awakened to life a cultural heritage that had been largely buried for a long time.... This occurred, on the one hand, by philological work; critical editions of sources called for the text-critical method in particular. It also became the prerequisite for biblical exegesis; the work of Erasmus on the New Testament is an important proof of this. Knowledge of biblical languages—now also increasingly Hebrew—was recognized as a decisive prerequisite for it" (Reventlow, *History of Biblical Interpretation*, 1).

5. Rendtorff's theology is a welcome exception to this general trend (*The Canonical Hebrew Bible*).

Introduction

absence of the Bible and the fractured foundations of biblical faith. The voice of Christianity has been reduced to a series of disparate sound bites lacking the biblical context needed to bolster and define its message.

The present volume is devoted to the Bible's textuality, the unique combination of literary genres that constitute the focus of both private and public faith and without which the people of God cannot continue to exist in any sort of recognizable way.[6] The Bible has a pre-history and in some cases an oral pre-history, but the Bible as it now stands is a literary phenomenon. Likewise, while the Bible is both historical and theological, it is not strictly speaking history or theology. It is literature. It is thus necessary to describe it in textual, literary, and even in linguistic terms. The biblical authors are remarkably self-aware of writing. As compared to Homer's the *Iliad* and the *Odyssey*, which refer to writing only once (in the *Iliad*), the Bible has 429 references to writing or written documents.[7] The biblical authors are also conscious of one another and are not shy about their mutual admiration and dependence. They wholeheartedly commend the textual nature of revelation to their readers. It is this very textuality that requires the church to be a people of the book, nothing more and nothing less.

---

6. Strictly speaking this is metadiscourse about the nature of the Bible, yet the distinctive shape of the canon drives the discussion. This kind of conscious reflection is necessary to maintain an awareness of what is so easily lost to those things that are on the periphery of the Bible.

7. Diringer, "Biblical Scripts," 13.

1

Orality and Textuality

THE RELATIONSHIP BETWEEN THE text(s) of the Bible and any possible oral traditions behind them has long been of interest to biblical scholars.[1] More recently, oral performance of texts has captured the attention of those seeking to explain the Bible in something other than strictly textual categories.[2] In addition to these issues is the matter of the dynamic quality of orality over against the potentially static textualization of that orality. This chapter is not intended to deny oral tradition/performance or the value of orality in general. Rather, it is an attempt to avoid the confusion of orality and textuality. Related to this discussion will be the treatment of other non-textual phenomena that frequently obscure the textuality of the Bible in interpretation. Of course, the goal is to give the Bible's textuality its proper place, but this will not be at the expense of other legitimate pursuits.

---

1. "If one is able to trace a text's origin and, if necessary, its formative changes back into the realm of oral tradition, then transmission history prepares indispensable insights for understanding this text. One can detect locality, time, rationale, and the arena of usage concerning the origin and the changes. Together with the transmission form's characteristic components these insights leave traces in oral tradition up to the oldest literary version of the text. Also, on the basis of this prehistory, these insights make the text understandable" (Steck, *Old Testament Exegesis*, 71). Steck's confidence in the assumed self-evident reliability of the process and methodology is apparent.

2. See, for example, the papers presented in the "Orality and Textuality" section of the recent annual meetings of the Society of Biblical Literature.

Oral Tradition

The Bible itself bears witness to the oral performance of stories, laws, prophecies, poems, and songs prior to their written form and prior to the inclusion of their written form within the larger composition of the biblical texts. The text of Judg 5:11 mentions the recounting of the righteous acts of YHWH, which now has a textual reference in the narratives of the Pentateuch (cf. 1 Sam 12:7). The laws at Sinai were delivered orally (Exod 20:1, 19; Deut 5:4–5) and only later were committed to writing (Exod 24:4, 12; 31:18; Deut 5:22). The sermons of the prophets (e.g., Jer 7) have been collected and textualized and thereby have been re-contextualized so that messages for past generations can now be messages for future generations.[3] As for the psalms, Hermann Gunkel attempted to reconstruct from their written forms the "setting in life" (*Sitz im Leben*) in which their content might have been uttered.[4] The sayings of the book of Proverbs also likely stem from larger oral and written traditions (1 Kgs 5:9–14 [Eng., 4:29–34]).[5]

But the assumption that this pre-history somehow explains the intended meaning of the currently extant literature is not necessarily a warranted one. Apart from the general uncertainty surrounding reconstruction of tradition and apart from a basic inability to access directly the oral performance of earlier traditions, there are issues that should prevent the interpreter from making too facile a correlation between orality and textuality even when confidence in the reconstruction is high. For example, the Sinai

---

3. Thus, the goal in interpretation of the prophetic books is not the sermon itself, as if the texts were mere transcripts, or even the prophet himself. "There is no 'real Amos' other than the one brokered by the text's discursive unfolding" (Seitz, *Prophecy and Hermeneutics*, 230). Likewise, there is no historical Jesus apart from the biblical Jesus. This is not to say that the one is at odds with the other. Rather, the biblical Jesus is a unique and revelatory theological interpretation of the life of Christ. Any attempt to reconstruct him independently either replaces or obscures the biblical portrait of him.

4. Gunkel and Begrich, *Introduction to the Psalms*.

5. See, in particular, the relationship between the sayings of the wise (Prov 22:17—24:22; 24:23–34) and the Egyptian instruction of Amenemopet (Pritchard, *Ancient Near Eastern Texts*, 421–25).

Orality and Textuality

law is now not only in written form, but also it is set within a larger narrative and compositional framework that provides its own context for interpretation. Likewise, while individual psalms may have had a life of their own in either oral or written form, they are now part of the book of Psalms where their relationship to other written psalms exerts an influence on how they are to be read. Even the rehearsals of biblical history (e.g., Deut 26:5-9; Josh 24:1-15; Ezek 20; Pss 78; 105; 106; 136; Neh 9), which are generally taken to be manifestations of variant oral and written traditions about Israel's history, are now presented to the reader as examples of textual exegesis.[6] Furthermore, appeals to extra-biblical tradition to explain texts like Hosea 12, which refers to the Jacob story, appear dubious and unnecessary compared to the abundant and firm textual evidence of Genesis.[7] Oral performance of texts prior to their inclusion within the composition of a biblical book would also belong to the pre-history of that book. On the other hand, oral performance of biblical books or portions thereof would belong to the subsequent history of reading and interpretation. Information about such performance could conceivably provide insight into the way the texts were copied, transmitted, and received. But it does not belong to the stage of biblical composition, which is a purely textual enterprise. Explanation of oral performance does not at the same time constitute explanation of the texts performed.

Writing in antiquity was special in part because the number of those who could produce and read substantial literary works was limited compared to the modern world (Isa 29:11-12).[8] Writ-

---

6. See Shepherd, *Textual World of the Bible*.

7. Shepherd, *Text in the Middle*. David Carr has recently argued for oral-written transmission of texts on the basis of perceived memory variants and on the basis of evidence for memorization of large portions of texts (*Formation of the Hebrew Bible*, 13-36). Apart from the possibility of other explanations such as textual interpretation and what might appear to be equally pristine readings (see Talmon, *Text and Canon*, 171-216; Tov, *Textual Criticism*, 163-65), the reality of a scribe alternating between a written source and his own memory is not always easy to conceptualize unless multiple sources are being referenced (e.g., the *Temple Scroll*).

8. "Reading and writing were restricted to a professional elite; the majority of the population was nonliterate" (Toorn, *Scribal Culture*, 1). "Sometimes

TEXTUALITY AND THE BIBLE

ing was not only a way to preserve words (e.g., Isa 8:16; Dan 8:26; 12:4; Rev 22:10) but also a way to lend authority and power to words.⁹ Thus, for example, Job's desire to have his words written (Job 19:23–24) might be more than a wish for the preservation of his argument for posterity. It may very well be a longing for an authoritative status that would strengthen his case for vindication.

On the other hand, there has always been resistance to writing at least in some circles and in particular circumstances. Those who are not members of the elite, literate class do not always find their voice represented in writing. Furthermore, some words are better spoken than written. The living voice of the teacher is in many ways just as valuable as the text.¹⁰ William Schniedewind has suggested that the reference to the "false pen of the scribes" in Jer 8:8 is an example of such an objection to textualization, although it is possible that the verse is a reference to tampering with actual texts, tampering evident even in the transmission of the book of Jeremiah when the MT and the LXX (cf. 4QJer$^{b,\ d}$) are compared.¹¹

Schniedewind also cites the critique of writing in the complaint of Plato's Socrates to Phaedrus: "Written words seem to talk to you as though they were intelligent, but if you ask them

---

scholars will refer to the number of times 'reading' and 'writing' is mentioned in the Hebrew Bible and assume that this demonstrates that elites and non-elites could read and write. However, I would contend that the Hebrew Bible was primarily a corpus written by elites to elites" (Rollston, *Writing and Literacy*, 133). "A number of scholars have argued that the biblical canon and its texts are rather more of a scribal creation than previously allowed. These scribes are also seen as an elite class, and inventive producers rather than transcribers of ideology" (Davies and Römer, *Writing the Bible*, 4).

9. See Schniedewind, *How the Bible Became a Book*, 24–34.

10. "Writing locates authority in a text and its reader instead of in a tradition and a community. Writing does not require the living voice. Thus, writing has the power to supplant traditional modes of teaching and social structures of education. In a pre-literate society authority was entirely dependent upon traditions held by parents and elders and passed down orally from generation to generation. The community held the keys to wisdom and authority. Written texts had *the possibility* of replacing traditional community-centered wisdom. One no longer had to depend on the community for knowledge and wisdom because the written word itself could confer knowledge" (ibid., 114).

11. Ibid., 115.

Orality and Textuality

anything about what they say, from a desire to be instructed, they go on telling you just the same thing forever. And once a thing is put in writing, the composition, whatever it may be, drifts all over the place" (*Phaedrus* §275d).[12] This quote highlights one of the key differences between orality and textuality.[13] The author of a text is not present to explain what he/she has written every time the text is read. A teacher, on the other hand, is present with the students and is available to interact with them over the content of the teaching. But what this means is that the author must put his text together with such considerations in mind, anticipating questions and objections from readers. Perhaps the real objection in the above citation is to the recording of teaching intended for a particular audience at a certain time. This would be comparable to the audio recording of a modern lecture. The lecture is really directed to the students who are in the moment and who share the context of the rest of the course. To isolate that lecture for someone who was not present would be to decontextualize the content. It is very difficult to freeze such a moment and make it transferable to other settings without significant loss. A consciously constructed literary work, however, is ideally prepared to be read by anyone. As for the unchangeable nature of such a literary work, it likely depends upon the quality of the content and the perspective of the reader as to whether or not its immutability is a positive or a negative.

Text and Reference

What about other non-textual phenomena behind the text of the Bible such as the many objects (people, places, things, and events), concepts, and ideas to which the Bible refers? Scholars often claim without argumentation that an independent account of such things helps the interpreter to understand the text. In actual fact,

---

12. Ibid., 14.

13. This is not to mention the many other differences such as the gestures, facial expressions, and intonation associated with spoken language that cannot be reproduced in written form.

the reason why these same scholars fail to connect the dots of this claim is that their independent accounts do not explain the meaning of the text at all. What their reconstructions do contribute, however, is an explanation of the things to which the Bible refers beyond what the Bible itself says.[14] This simply requires an understanding of the way in which language works and its relationship to reality.

Hans Frei's monumental work, *The Eclipse of Biblical Narrative*, keenly identifies the emergence of preoccupation with the historicity of the Bible in the post-Reformation period. This historicity of the Bible or the lack thereof became separable from the Bible itself so that the Bible's own account was either questioned or defended on the grounds of independent historical reconstructions. These reconstructions then took the place of explication of biblical narrative. For skeptics, an account of "what really happened" sufficed as an explanation of the biblical text. Conservatives conceded this playing ground and responded not with the unique contribution of the biblical narrative itself but with an elaborate defense of the Bible's historicity largely on the basis of extra-biblical information. Once this defense was complete, the Bible had been "explained." The Bible's textual representation of reality was rendered irrelevant.[15] It is not difficult to find manifestations of this eclipse in virtually every form of biblical interpretation today.[16]

---

14. James Barr makes this point well in a discussion of Leviathan in the book of Job: "The primary need of the exegete is not to 'identify' the mythological background, in the sense of stating exactly what pre-existing myth is presupposed; what is more important is the myth as it is reconstructed by the poet for his own purposes.... The pre-Israelite background is interesting information, but is not more than ancillary to the explanation of the passage" (*Comparative Philology*, 382–83).

15. Criticism of this approach has somehow resulted in accusations of the denial of the historical events. But this need not necessarily follow. It is at its core a clarification of the object of study.

16. A classic example of the lasting effect of the eclipse is the following statement from a widely used conservative introduction to the Old Testament: "... the exodus was God's greatest act of salvation in the Old Testament" (Longman and Dillard, *Introduction to the OT*, 72–73). This confusion between the

Orality and Textuality

Largely due to the influence of modern linguistics, biblical scholars have come to recognize the referential fallacy in word studies, as the following quote from James Barr so amply illustrates:

> Students may find it helpful to use the distinction between reference and information. By 'reference' I mean that to which a word refers, the actual thought or entity which is its referent. By 'information' I mean the difference which is conveyed, within a known and recognized sign system (a language like Hebrew or Arabic), by the fact that it is *this* sign and not another that is used. The major linguistic interest, it would seem to me, lies in the latter. Many arguments in which biblical scholars adduce linguistic evidence appear to me, however, to involve some confusion between the former and the latter.[17]

Barr uses the example of an attempt to define the word *maqom* ("place") as "tomb" simply on the grounds that in some passages it refers to a tomb. But words are not defined by the things to which they refer. Rather, things are described by words.

The relationship between "words" (*verba*) and "things" (*res*) is an arbitrary one.[18] Words are defined on the basis of their usage within the language and on the basis of their relationship to other words within the same semantic field.[19] Thus, an independent

---

history of ancient Israel and the text of the Hebrew Scriptures is all too common and results in a loss of meaning and significance. It can certainly be said that the original exodus from Egypt was God's greatest act of salvation in the history of ancient Israel, but the greatest act of salvation revealed in the text of the Hebrew Bible is the new exodus (e.g., Num 23:22; 24:8; Isa 11:16; 43:16-21; Hos 2:16-17 [Eng., 2:14-15]; Mic 7:15). The same can be said of the overly simplistic identification of the Hebrew Bible with the law, the old covenant, or Judaism, resulting in a fundamental inability to see any genuine continuity with the New Testament documents.

17. Barr, *Comparative Philology*, 291-92.

18. See Ernesti, *Institutio interpretis Novi Testamenti*, 8; Saussure, *Cours de Linguistique Générale*, 67-69. Ernesti argued that this relationship excluded any attempt to explain words from the things to which they refer. He insisted that it should be the other way around. Words acquire meaning by custom.

19. See Barr, *Semantics of Biblical Language*. Barr's approach has been adopted in *TLOT*: "*TLOT* has consciously not been planned as a reference work for comparative religion or archaeology, because the latter would shift

description of Rebekah (the referent) in Genesis 24 does not explain the meaning of the terms *naarah* ("a young female"), *bethulah* ("a young woman who has not conceived"), and *almah* ("a young woman of marriageable age who does not have a husband") that refer to Rebekah, nor does it explain their relationship to one another or why the author would choose one or the other. Now the challenge is to have scholars recognize the referential fallacy not only with individual words but also with phrases, clauses, and whole texts.

Perhaps more than any else, John Sailhamer has drawn attention to the importance of making this distinction, especially with regard to the importance of the text as the locus of revelation in evangelical doctrine (2 Tim 3:16).[20] Sailhamer fully affirms the historicity of the events referenced in the Bible and the significance of those real events for Christian faith (1 Cor 15:14), but he is also concerned to allow the unique textual depiction of the events maintain its voice lest the interpreter's contributions from outside the text obscure the specific theological rendering intended by the authors. Sailhamer uses the illustration of a Rembrandt painting to make his point:

> Using modern historical tools, we have the same ability to fill in the historical details of seventeenth-century life over the shadows of a Rembrandt painting. By painting shadows, Rembrandt deliberately left out many historical details that would have given us much information about the events he recorded on canvas. Historians who understand the culture and life setting of seventeenth-century Europe could easily replace Rembrandt's dark shadows with historically accurate details of the world around him . . . We should not seek to know what lies behind or beneath Rembrandt's shadows. It is the shadows that are a central part of the paintings, not the historical details that lie behind the shadows and are thus not in the

---

the major emphasis (similar to that of a theological dictionary) too heavily from the semantic function of words to the description of the referent and its history" (Jenni and Westermann, *TLOT*, xv).

20. Sailhamer, *Introduction to OT Theology*, 36–85.

Orality and Textuality

painting. Rembrandt's meaning lies as much in what is not seen in his painting as in what is seen. The shadows, by blocking out the irrelevant details, help us focus on what is seen. The effect of our adding more details to the painting would be to lose Rembrandt's focus.[21]

If forced to make a choice, would it be preferable to be present at an event like the exodus or the crucifixion, or would it be preferable to have the biblical depiction and interpretation of those events? Many would jump at the opportunity to be present at the events themselves, not realizing that the events are not self-interpreting even though they are inherently meaningful. Thus, someone present at the exodus would certainly have a sense of the power of God, but would that person know about the new exodus? Someone present at the crucifixion would know that Jesus died, but would that person know that Jesus died for the sins of the world? Only the Bible provides that information.[22]

---

21. Sailhamer, *Meaning of the Pentateuch*, 104. For Sailhamer, following Ernesti, the "historical" sense is the "grammatical" sense (ibid., 100–148).

22. For further reading, see Schmidt, *Contextualizing Israel's Sacred Writings*.

2

Self-aware Bookishness

AMONG THE MANY REFERENCES to writing in the Bible is a pervasive self-awareness of the bookmaking process and the importance of textualization. Such conscious reflection on the Bible's own bookishness and the authority attached to it comes across as part of the author's message to the reader. That is, there is an implicit invitation to embrace composition and intertextuality as God's chosen means of revelation. This ranges from the residue of the composition process such as the *toledoth* formula in Genesis (Gen 2:4; 5:1; 6:9; 10:1; 11:10, 27; 25:12, 19; 36:1, 9; 37:2) and the scribal colophons in Leviticus (Lev 7:35–38; 11:46–47; 12:7b; 13:59; 14:32, 54–56; 15:32–33; 23:37–38; 26:46; 27:34) to the practice of inner-biblical exegesis. Here the focus will be on the occurrence of source citation and the more or less direct references to book production and the commendation thereof. Reconstruction of hypothetical sources such as those of the documentary hypothesis are not the interest of this chapter.

Pentateuch and Former Prophets

While the account of the stone tablets written by the finger of God would seem to be an appropriate starting point for this section (Exod 31:18), the story is not about the inclusion of the Decalogue within the text and composition of the Pentateuch. Rather, the explicit source citation in Num 21:14–15 is more along the lines of what the following discussion will include. The reference in Num

Self-aware Bookishness

21:14 is to "the Book of the Wars of YHWH," a no longer extant source not cited anywhere else. The citation draws an inference from the surrounding context about Israel's travels, although, as the variation in both ancient and modern translations shows, the exact content of the citation is not entirely clear.[1] Given the possible poetic (or at least parallelistic) quality of the passage, there may be a relationship to the songs in Num 21:17-18, 27-30. What is important for the present discussion, however, is the fact that the author/composer makes his use of pre-existing sources explicit and thus reveals something of great value to the reader of the Pentateuch. The book consists of a wide variety of material (narratives, poems, genealogies, laws, etc.) from different times and places now woven together into a coherent whole.[2] The task of the reader is to discern not only the meaning of clauses (microstructures) but also the grammar of the juxtaposition of these larger swaths of material (macrostructures).[3]

---

1. See Christensen, "Num 21:14-15 and the Book," 359-60. Note in particular the rendering of Num 21:14 in *Targum Neofiti*: "Therefore, written and specified (or, interpreted) in the book of the Torah of the Lord, which is compared to the Book of the Wars, are the signs and mighty deeds that the Lord performed with Israel when they were standing by the Sea of Reeds, and the mighty deeds that he performed with them when they were crossing the Arnon" (cf. *Tg. Ps.-J.*). See also the LXX.

2. This method of composition is well known from the ancient Near East as the following comment about the integration of the Akkadian episodes of Gilgamesh makes clear: "... the integration was not simply an act of compilation, whereby separate episodes about a single character were mechanically placed together in sequence, but rather, as Kramer held, a careful process of revision. In this process, the original episodes were modified by certain deliberate changes that cemented them together in the service of a particular theme that the epic develops. The plan of the integrated epic thus testifies to the working of a single artistic mind, and the work of this person is so creative that he deserves to be considered an *author*, rather than an editor or compiler" (Tigay, *Evolution of the Gilgamesh Epic*, 42).

3. This in no way detracts from the doctrines of inspiration and inerrancy. What makes the Bible revelatory is the final combination of texts, not the content of the pre-existing sources that the author has now adopted for his own purposes. The biblical doctrine of inspiration asserts that the texts are inspired (2 Tim 3:16) and that the authors were carried along by the Holy Spirit (2 Pet 1:21). It does not delineate the mode of composition. This has to

Deuteronomy is well known for its interest in the writing (Deut 31:9) and the copying (Deut 17:18; 27:3) of the Torah. Moses preserved the Torah in writing so that each subsequent generation could learn the fear of YHWH (Deut 31:9-13; cf. Neh 8-9). His instructions for the king (Deut 17:14-20) included the making of a copy of the Torah to read it publicly in accordance with Deut 31:9-13 in order to teach the fear of YHWH (cf. 2 Kgs 22-23). The command to write the words of the Torah on stones (Deut 27:1-8) was followed by Joshua (Josh 8:30-35). But Joshua also had "the book of the Torah," which was to be the object of his private reading (Josh 1:8; cf. Ps 1:2). His speech in Josh 24:1-15 is the product of his reflection on this book, an attempt to locate the events of his own day within the framework of the biblical narrative.[4]

The book of Joshua also refers to "the Book of Jashar" (Josh 10:13; cf. 2 Sam 1:18; LXX 1 Kgs 8:13, 53a). The word *jashar* (or, *yashar*) means "upright," but because the material cited from this source is always poetic, some have suggested a slight adjustment to the consonantal text to make it the book of *shir* ("song"), as reflected in LXX 1 Kgs 8:53a.[5] The reading in Josh 10:13 is somewhat suspect since the LXX does not contain the reference to this source. The LXX of Joshua represents a Hebrew edition of the book that is about four to five percent shorter than the MT, yet it also features some significant pluses (Josh 16:10; 19:47; 21:42; 24:30, 33). As it now stands in the MT, the material cited from the Book of Jashar is a poetic depiction of the narrative of Joshua's divinely

---

be determined organically from the texts themselves. See Driver, *Introduction to the Literature of the OT*, xi.

4. According to Josh 24:26, Joshua wrote the words of an agreement between him and the people in "the book of the Torah of God." Jewish tradition asserts that "Joshua wrote the book that is called by his name and the last eight verses of the Torah" (*b. B. Bat.* 14b). It is doubtful whether the words of the agreement refer to the entire book of Joshua, and there is no account of it in the Torah. Thus, it is possible that the understanding reflected in Josh 24:26 is that the book of Joshua, which includes the agreement, is in many ways a continuation of the story of Moses in the Torah, which concluded with his death account.

5. The Syriac Peshitta renders it "the Book of Praises." *Targum Jonathan* calls it the book of the Torah (cf. *Tg. Neof.* Num 21:14; *Tg. J.* 2 Sam 1:18).

enabled defense of the Gibeonites against the southern coalition of kings in which Joshua went up "all night" from Gilgal (Josh 10:9) and did not finish the job until the sunset of the following day (Josh 10:27), giving the impression of a longer-than-usual day in which the luminaries were halted.

The text cited from the Book of Jashar in 2 Sam 1:18 is a song entitled the "Bow" (2 Sam 1:22) that David taught the sons of Judah when he lamented the deaths of Saul and Jonathan.[6] This lament (2 Sam 1:19–27) plays a significant role in the composition of the book of Samuel. Along with the major poetic units at the beginning of 1 Samuel (1 Sam 2:1–10) and at the end of 2 Samuel (2 Sam 22:1—23:7), the poem serves to guide the reader in the interpretation of the narrative. David's respect for Saul's office and his covenant relationship with Jonathan prove to be genuine in the wake of their deaths, setting the stage for his dealings with the house of Saul and Jonathan in the subsequent narrative.

The reference to the Book of Jashar (actually, "the Book of Song") in 1 Kgs 8:13, 53a occurs in the LXX but not in the MT.[7] Not all witnesses to the LXX have 1 Kgs 8:12–13, but 1 Kgs 8:53a, which is not in the MT, appears to be the displaced (or, appended) poem that Solomon utters at the dedication of the temple and in response to the appearance of YHWH's glory (1 Kgs 8:11; cf. Exod 40:35). Much like the poems in the book of Samuel, the speech of Solomon plays a crucial role in the overall composition of the Former Prophets. The author/composer uses the words of his major

---

6. Here the Syriac renders "the Book of Jashar" as "the Book of Asher."

7. This would then be the opposite of Josh 10:13, which had the source citation in the MT but not in the LXX. Why do the biblical authors not cite their sources consistently? Such a question assumes the modern era in which matters of copyright and plagiarism loom large. In antiquity, to include preexisting material in a new and original way was not only a complement to the author of the source but also a sign of the composer's skill. The edges of cited material are often discernible without explicit reference, but the biblical authors do provide enough citation to establish the practice beyond the shadow of a doubt.

protagonists as his own mouthpiece to reflect on the meaning of the stories that precede them (cf. Josh 24; 1 Sam 12).[8]

Jewish tradition assigns the book of Samuel to Samuel himself (*b. B. Bat.* 14b), even though his character dies halfway through the narrative (1 Sam 25:1; 28:3). The present form of the book presupposes a time later than that of Samuel (1 Sam 9:9; 27:6; 2 Sam 13:18; 19:44). Having said this, there are two references to Samuel's writing activity that seem to credit him with at least part of what can be read in the book (1 Sam 10:25; 1 Chr 29:29). According to 1 Sam 10:25, Samuel wrote in the *sefer* "the ordinance (*mishpat*) of the kingdom," which is apparently a reference to "the ordinance (*mishpat*) of the king" in 1 Sam 8:11–18 (cf. Deut 17:14–20). It is not clear from the context whether this *sefer* was a small scroll containing only the ordinance or a larger document with other material. In any case, the importance of this document is evident from its placement "before YHWH" (1 Sam 10:25), which may very well be a reference to the ark (cf. Exod 16:34).

Neither Samuel nor Kings cites a source for the stories of David, but this is supplied by the Chronicler in 1 Chr 29:29, which refers to the former and latter things of David written in the words of Samuel, Nathan, and Gad. It would seem that the Chronicler primarily had in mind the stories about David in Samuel and Kings that include these three prophets, not only because the Chronicler drew on these stories for his own work but also because he names them in the order in which they appear in the biblical narrative.[9] It is not certain, however, that the Chronicler intended to say that the material about David in Samuel and Kings came from a source or sources produced separately or jointly by Samuel, Nathan, and Gad. It is at least worth noting that source citation in the book of Samuel is not nearly as extensive and consistent as it is in Kings and Chronicles.

---

8. "In particular, at all the important points in the course of the history, Dtr. brings forward the leading personages with a speech, long or short which looks forward and backward in an attempt to interpret the course of events, and draws the relevant practical conclusions about what people should do" (Noth, *Deuteronomistic History*, 5).

9. Curtis and Madsen, *Critical and Exegetical Commentary*, 307–8.

Self-aware Bookishness

The book of Kings cites three main sources in its conclusions to the individual accounts of the kings of the north and the south in addition to the death notices and the indications of the kings' successors: the chronicles of Solomon (1 Kgs 11:41), the chronicles of the kings of Israel (1 Kgs 14:19), and the chronicles of the kings of Judah (1 Kgs 14:29).[10] These conclusions along with the formulaic introductions to the individual accounts, which compare the kings of the north to Jeroboam and those of the south to David, serve to guide the reader by demarcating the subsections of the larger work. While the chronicles of the kings of Israel and those of the kings of Judah are cited repeatedly throughout the book, the chronicles of Solomon are only referenced once at the end of his story. The corresponding source citation in the book of Chronicles (2 Chr 9:29) refers to the words of the prophets Nathan, Ahijah (1 Kgs 11:29), and Iddo (1 Kgs 13), although this citation does not appear in the Syriac version of Chronicles. It is not clear what the relationship might be between the words of these prophets and the chronicles of Solomon, but there is significant overlap between the cited content about Solomon in both books. In some ways the names of the sources represent two perspectives on the book of Kings—either a book about the kings or a book about the prophets who accompanied them. The book of Chronicles does cite a greater variety of sources than the book of Kings, including more prophetic sources (e.g., 2 Chr 32:32).

It is generally agreed that the author/composer of the book of Kings consistently cites his sources in order to lend credence to the historical veracity of his work and to direct his readers to the publicly accessible documents where facts could be checked and where more information about the kings could be found. This becomes an even greater matter for the Chronicler against whom the charge of revisionist history makes little sense in light of his extensive source citation. The author of Kings is so vigilant in maintaining

---

10. The story in 1 Kgs 14:1–20 appears in a different version without source citation in LXX 1 Kgs 12:24g–n. The LXX of 1 Kings represents a secondarily rearranged Hebrew edition of the book. See Tov, "Septuagint as a Source," 44–48.

the integrity of his sources that he leaves intact descriptions that would have no longer applied in his day (e.g., 1 Kgs 8:8; 2 Kgs 25; cf. Josh 4:9; Ps 72:20). What happened to these sources over the course of time? There is no certain answer to this question, but one possibility is that the unique selection of material in the books of Kings and Chronicles was seen as a fitting replacement for the older sources not only because those books chronicled the events accurately but also because they gave a definitive theological interpretation of the events.

Latter Prophets

Perhaps no biblical book displays more self-conscious reflection on its own process of composition than the prophetic book of Jeremiah.[11] To follow the clues to this process within the book is to sit in the very workshop of the priest-prophet-scribe himself. And there is even more clarity when the two editions of Jeremiah represented by the LXX (and 4QJer[b, d]) and the MT are compared and contrasted. The superscription in Jer 1:1–3 (cf. Isa 1:1) serves to introduce the book in its entirety as "the words of Jeremiah" (or, LXX: "the word of God that came to Jeremiah") and indicates the span of Jeremiah's prophetic ministry. Yet the present form of the book includes an appendix in chapter 52, which the MT clearly states does not belong to "the words of Jeremiah" (Jer 51:64b; cf. Jer 48:47b). That this notice does not appear in the LXX is due in part to the fact that chapters 46–51 appear in a different arrangement after Jer 25:13 in the edition of the book represented by that translation.

The first half of the book of Jeremiah concludes with these words: "And I will bring upon that land all my words that I spoke about it, all that is written in this book (*sefer*)" (Jer 25:13). The remainder of the verse ("which Jeremiah prophesied concerning all the nations") is in the LXX the heading for the collection of oracles addressed to the nations that follows at this juncture in its *Vorlage*.

---

11. See Holladay, *Jeremiah 2*, 16–20.

Self-aware Bookishness

The contents of the "book" referenced in Jer 25:13 is the subject of much speculation by scholars, but within the present form of the book of Jeremiah it refers to nothing other than what the reader has read thus far. A detailed account of the making of this "book" occurs in Jeremiah 36. In the fourth year of Jehoiakim (cf. Jer 25:1), Jeremiah dictated a "scroll" (*meghillath sefer*) to his scribe, Baruch (Jer 36:1–8). Baruch gave at a later time (MT: "in the fifth year"; LXX: "in the eighth year") a public reading of the scroll (Jer 36:9–13) and subsequently read it to the leaders who then advised both Baruch and Jeremiah to go into hiding before they communicated the contents of the scroll to the king (Jer 36:14–19).

The scroll itself was deposited in the chamber of Elishama the scribe while the words of the scroll were told to the king (Jer 36:20). The king commanded Jehudi to bring in the scroll to be read, but after the reading of three or four columns the king would tear the scroll and throw into the fire until it was completely destroyed (Jer 36:21–26), an action that stood in stark contrast to the response of Jehoiakim's father Josiah who tore his clothes when he heard the words of the book of the Torah (2 Kgs 22:11). There was, however, a rewriting of the scroll (Jer 36:27–32) with many words added (Jer 36:32b). This last part of the story provides invaluable insight into the growth and development of the book. Not only was the scroll rewritten, but also many words were added to it. The account in Jeremiah 36 is also referenced in Jer 45:1 in an introduction to a very brief chapter about Baruch's struggles as Jeremiah's scribe and God's response that he has graciously spared Baruch's life. This chapter is the last of the main part of the book before the appendix in the LXX and may have at one time served as the conclusion or scribal colophon to the "book" referenced in Jer 25:13.

Two other passages in Jeremiah mention "books" that now constitute substantial subunits within the overall composition of the prophet's work.[12] In Jer 30:2, YHWH instructs Jeremiah to write the words that he speaks in a "book" (*sefer*). This book includes the words of restoration found in chapters 30–31 and is

---

12. Jeremiah 29 contains a written "letter" (*sefer*) from Jeremiah to the exiles in Babylon.

now supplemented by chapters 32–33 in the final composition of the book of Jeremiah. The book mentioned in Jer 51:60 contains the words against Babylon in chapters 50–51. It is possible that this book also included the words directed to the other nations in Jeremiah 46–49. This option appears more likely in the MT arrangement where the reference to the book appears at the end of the collection of oracles to the nations. On the other hand, the placement of these oracles in the LXX in a different order after Jer 25:13 would seem to limit the scope to the words against Babylon.

Other prophetic books certainly bear the marks of composition such as the headings in Isaiah (Isa 2:1; 13:1), the date formulae in Ezekiel, or the material shared among the prophets or between the prophets and other biblical authors (e.g., 2 Kgs 18–20 and Isa 36–39; Isa 15–16 and Jer 48).[13] The Book of the Twelve is an example of twelve clearly discernible smaller compositions having undergone a process of inclusion within a larger work.[14] This process affected the way the smaller parts were read in antiquity.[15] But while these books do not hide the clues to their composition or their consciousness of the larger canon (e.g., Mal 3:22 [4:4]), they do not share the same self-awareness of their composition that the book of Jeremiah has. One possible exception to this is the mention of a "book of remembrance" in Mal 3:16. At first glance this would seem to be a metaphor for God's memory of the elect (cf. Exod 32:32; Isa 4:3; Dan 12:1; Rev 20:12–15), and that may very well be all that it is. But the placement of the reference to this book at the end of the composition of the Twelve at the very least suggests the possibility that the "book of remembrance" is the Book of the Twelve.

---

13. See Rendtorff, "Zur Komposition des Buches Jesaja," 295–320.

14. See Shepherd, "Compositional Analysis," 184–93; Shepherd, "New Exodus in the Composition."

15. Shepherd, *Twelve Prophets in the NT*.

The Writings

The signs of large-scale composition beyond the level of the individual psalm are evident in the doxologies that conclude the first four books of Psalms (Ps 41:14 [Eng., 41:13]; 72:18-19; 89:53 [Eng., 89:52]; 106:48). The double Amen that occurs at the end of these (Ps 41:14; 72:19; 89:53; 106:48 [LXX]) apparently had its influence on early post-biblical composition as attested by 4QShir^b, a scroll that ends with a double Amen. These markers preserved the boundaries of the book well as evidenced by the early translation of the LXX. Although the Greek text combines the individual psalms differently and adds a Psalm 151, the superscription to this last psalm is quick to note that it is "outside the number" (but see 11QPs^a). As with other biblical compositions, the author/composer of the final form book of Psalms did not hesitate to preserve earlier stages of the book's development (e.g., Ps 72:20). Perhaps the sentiment of Ps 45:2b (Eng., 45:1b) reflects that of the composer himself: "My tongue is a stylus of a skilled scribe (*sofer mahir*)" (cf. Ezra 7:6).[16]

The major collections in the book of Proverbs are well marked by superscriptions (Prov 1:1; 10:1; 22:17; 24:23; 25:1; 30:1; 31:1).[17] The heading in Prov 25:1 introduces a collection of Solomon's proverbs, which the men of Hezekiah "copied/transcribed/transmitted" (*hetiqu*). The precise meaning of this latter term is uncertain, although it is generally agreed that it refers to some scribal activity of "advancing" the proverbs of Solomon. For the present purposes, it is of particular importance to note that the current form of this collection does not come directly from Solomon. In fact, the role of these men of Hezekiah was so highly regarded in

---

16. This is an interesting thought in light of the discussion of orality and textuality in chapter 1. The psalms are often considered in terms of their "original" oral setting, yet the writing psalmist does not compare his stylus to a skilled tongue. Rather, the skilled scribe is the standard of excellence to which he compares his own tongue. The spoken language aspires to that of the written language.

17. The book of Sirach follows the model of concluding the book with an acrostic poem about a woman (Prov 31:10-31; Sir 51:13-30).

Jewish tradition (*b. B. Bat.* 15a) that the composition of several other biblical books, including the entire book of Proverbs, was attributed to them (Isaiah, Song of Songs, and Ecclesiastes).[18]

The epilogue/colophon to Ecclesiastes features the author's reflection on Qoheleth's scribal practices (Eccl 12:9–11) as well as some comments on the general enterprise of bookmaking (Eccl 12:12–14).[19] According to Eccl 12:9b, Qoheleth "weighed and sought, he arranged many sayings." He was a wise man (i.e., sage), a master of collections of such sayings (Eccl 12:11). Yet the author felt the need to warn his son/pupil of the fact that there is no end to the making of books such as these (Eccl 12:12). Excessive devotion to such bookmaking ultimately wears on the body. The reader gets the impression that Qoheleth could have gone on indefinitely without resolution. Thus, the author provides his own conclusion and evaluation, commending to his readers the fear of God (cf. Job 28:28; Prov 1:7; 9:10) in light of the final judgment (Eccl 12:13–14).

The book of Lamentations does not reflect on its own process of composition, although the acrostic structuring of the individual chapters is apparent to any reader of the Hebrew text.[20] Early post-biblical interpretation attributed the book's composition to Jeremiah (LXX; *Tg. J.*). The book of Esther mentions the writing and sending of letters from Mordecai and Esther to their people (Esth 9:20–32), but this is not a reference to authorship of the book of Esther (*contra* Rashi). Rather, these were letters sent to establish the feast of Purim (cf. Esth 1:22; 3:12–15; 8:10–14). The conclusion to the book contains a source citation similar to what is found in Kings and Chronicles when it refers to "the book of the chronicles of the kings of Media and Persia" (Esth 10:2; cf. LXX Esth 10).

The composite nature of the book of Daniel is evident from its use of two different languages: Hebrew (Dan 1:1—2:4a; 8–12)

---

18. The Song of Songs is a noteworthy example out of this group whose title (*shir hashshirim*) may very well denote not only that the book is the best song but also that it is a song made of multiple songs (see Longman, *Song of Songs*, 87–88).

19. See Fishbane, *Biblical Interpretation*, 29–31.

20. See Shepherd, "Hebrew Acrostic Poems," 95–108.

Self-Aware Bookishness

and Aramaic (Dan 2:4b—7:28). In spite of efforts to explain this phenomenon according to theories of translation, the manuscript evidence suggests that these were the languages in which the final composer found these texts when he put them together.[21] The book itself is self-conscious of its own bilingualism, inserting a scribal note at the end of Dan 2:4a, *aramith*, which the NET translates in brackets, "What follows is in Aramaic" (cf. LXX; *syristi*; 1QDan^a; Ezra 4:7). In addition to this, the angel in Dan 12:4 instructs Daniel to close the words and seal them in a "book" (*sefer*). While the placement of this instruction toward the end of the book might suggest an attempt to attribute the entire composition to Daniel (cf. Rev 22:10), the use of similar language in Dan 8:26b indicates that it may only refer to the contents of the vision in Daniel 10–12.[22]

While the book of Ezra-Nehemiah clearly has its distinct parts (e.g., Neh 1:1a), the combined work features key repetition (Ezra 2; Neh 7), overlap (Neh 8:9; 12:26, 36), and temporal sequencing (Ezra 1:1; 7:7; Neh 1:1; 2:1). The book also contains original letters of correspondence in Aramaic, the *lingua franca* of the Persian Empire (Ezra 4:8—6:18; 7:12–26).[23] But perhaps more important for the present discussion is the description of Ezra the scribe as a biblical scholar (Ezra 7:6, 10), which is something the reader has not encountered thus far. He functions in this role in the community (Ezra 9–10), reading and explaining the Torah to the people (Neh 8–9). Ezra was a "skilled scribe" (*sofer mahir*; cf. Ps 45:2) in the Torah of Moses (Ezra 7:6). According to Ezra 7:10, Ezra not only studied and taught the Torah, he also "made/composed" (*asah*) it. A comparison with the terminology of Eccl 12:12 suggests that this does not mean Ezra merely practiced the

---

21. See Shepherd, *Verbal System of Biblical Aramaic*, 10–18; Shepherd, *Daniel in the Context*, 66–67. It is also worth noting that Aramaic Targums were not made for only two books of the Hebrew Bible: Daniel and Ezra-Nehemiah. This was presumably because these were the only two books that contained substantial portions of Aramaic material. If Dan 2:4b–7:28 was not originally in Aramaic, why was no Targum produced?

22. Daniel's reading of a corpus of prophetic scriptures in Dan 9:2 will fall within the purview of the discussion in chapter 3.

23. Cf. 2 Kgs 18:26.

Torah, as it is usually translated, but that he had an active hand in composing the present form of the Torah (see *b. Sanh.* 21b).[24] This would explain the post-exilic perspective of non-Mosaic parts of the Torah like Deut 34:5–12, which looks back over the history of Israel's prophets (Deut 34:10) and connects the Torah to the rest of the canon (Deut 34:9–10; Josh 1:8; Mal 3:22–24 [Eng., 4:4–6]; Ps 1:2).

The book of Chronicles features the longest list of sources, but this does not mean that the Chronicler was a mere compiler. A comparison with Genesis–Kings shows that he was an exegete and theologian in his own right. The first formal source citations occur in 1 Chr 9:1 (see also 1 Chr 4:22) and 1 Chr 29:29, which was mentioned above in the discussion of Samuel. There is also a reference to the written blueprints for the temple that David gave to Solomon in 1 Chr 28:12–19. This passage is not in the Syriac version. Of particular interest is the claim that the text came from YHWH himself (1 Chr 28:19). The source for the Solomon material is cited in 2 Chr 9:29 (cf. 1 Kgs 11:41).

When the reader turns to the stories of the kings of Judah, the Chronicler does not simply cite the chronicles of the kings of Judah as in the book of Kings, although clearly the sources bear some sort of relationship to one another given the general overlap between them. In some cases it may be a matter of identical sources by different names. In others the situation might be that of different sources with shared material. The stories in Chronicles are often attributed to the prophets. For example, the account of Rehoboam comes from "the words of Shemaiah the prophet and Iddo the seer" (2 Chr 12:15; cf. 1 Kgs 12:22; 14:29; 2 Chr 9:29).[25] The story of Abijah is cited from "the *midrash* of the prophet Iddo" (2 Chr 13:22; cf. 1 Kgs 15:7). The use of the term *midrash* ("interpretation") may provide some insight into the nature of these sources.[26]

---

24. See the books attributed to Ezra and the Men of the Great Assembly in *Avot.* 1:1; *b. B. Bat.* 15a.

25. Note that 2 Chr 11:1—12:12 is not in the Syriac version.

26. Later rabbinic literature made a distinction between *peshat* ("simple

Self-aware Bookishness

Several citations refer to books of kings whose precise relationship to one another or to the biblical book of Kings is not entirely clear: "the book of the kings of Judah and of Israel" (2 Chr 16:11; 25:26; 28:26), "the words of Jehu the son of Hanani that are taken up in the book of the kings of Israel" (2 Chr 20:34; see 1 Kgs 16:1, 7, 12; 2 Chr 19:2), "the *midhrash* of the book of kings" (2 Chr 24:27), "the book of the kings of Israel and Judah" (2 Chr 27:7; 35:27; 36:8), "the prophetic vision of Isaiah the son of Amoz, the prophet and the book of the kings of Judah and Israel" (2 Chr 32:32; cf. Isa 1:1; 2 Chr 26:22), and "the words of the kings of Israel" and "the words of his [Manasseh's] seers" (2 Chr 33:18-19; cf. LXX).

The accounts of Asa (2 Chr 14-16) and Jehoshaphat (2 Chr 17-20) are considerably expanded when compared to the book of Kings (1 Kgs 15:9-24; 1 Kgs 22:41-51). The story of Hezekiah (2 Chr 29-32) is also remarkably different from what appears in 2 Kings 18-20 and Isaiah 36-39, the two sources apparently cited in 2 Chr 32:32. It is only chapter 32 of 2 Chronicles that contains an abbreviated version of the Hezekiah story found in those sources. The prophet Isaiah is also mentioned as a source for the Uzziah story in 2 Chr 26:22, calling to mind the reference to Uzziah in Isa 6:1. The story of Manasseh comes from two different sources (2 Chr 33:18-19), although there is some overlap between them. Both sources include his prayer (2 Chr 33:12-13), which is not part of the story in the book of Kings (2 Kgs 21). The words of the seers are in the words of the kings of Israel (2 Chr 33:18). Manasseh's sin and treachery and the places where he built cultic sites and erected Asherah poles and idols are written in the words of his seers (2 Chr 33:19).

---

interpretation") and *derash* ("imaginative interpretation"). Modern scholarship generally uses the term *midhrash* to refer to an actualizing type of exegesis. But in antiquity the term was an all-encompassing one for interpretation (see Neusner, *Introduction to Rabbinic Literature*, 225). It was the product of the verbal action in *darash* ("study"; Ezra 7:10).

The New Testament

The compositional structuring of the Gospels and Acts is generally well marked (e.g., Matt 7:28; 11:1; 13:53; 19:1; 26:1). Luke offers some thoughts in his addresses to Theophilus on the process and purpose behind his own writing of the story (Luke 1:1-4; Acts 1:1-5). His use of speeches to punctuate the narrative in Acts is reminiscent of the same compositional technique in the Former Prophets. But it is John's purpose statement (John 20:30-31) that stands apart in its reflection on writing. John first indicates that Jesus did many other things not written in the present book. In fact, the final verse of the book goes on to suggest that to include in writing all that Jesus did would be impossibly voluminous (John 21:25). So it is important to note that John's work is selective, as is the work of any other writer or composer. That is, the reader must allow the author to say certain things and not to say certain other things. When the reader disregards the author's selectivity and begins to fill in the gaps arbitrarily, he or she loses sight of the author's purpose.[27] In this case, the author's purpose is life-giving belief that the Christ known from the Hebrew Scriptures is the historical Jesus of Nazareth selectively presented in the book toward this end.[28] John has explained the life, death, and resurrection of Jesus from the Hebrew Scriptures by means of composition of selected words and deeds (e.g., John 1:45; 5:46). Of course, John is known for his purpose statements elsewhere (1 John 1:4; 5:13) and his general awareness of the weight and significance of his work for his readers (Rev 1:3; cf. Ps 1).

Paul's letters feature several references to writing or writings, although some of these apply more to canon consciousness (e.g., 2 Tim 3:16) than to what might be called self-aware bookishness. The complexity of the Corinthian correspondence is well known. Within 1 and 2 Corinthians there are references to a previous letter (1 Cor 5:9; 2 Cor 6:14—7:1?) and a severe letter (2 Cor 2:3-4; 7:8, 12; 2 Cor 10-13?). Paul's letters to the Ephesians and the Colossians

---

27. See Sternberg, *Poetics of Biblical Narrative*, 186-229.
28. See Carson, "Syntactical and Text-Critical Observations," 693-714.

Self-aware Bookishness

are cognate in many ways and subject to textual comparison. There is a reference to an exchange of letters between the Colossians and the Laodiceans (Col 4:16), suggesting that Paul never intended his letters to be so particular to an "original" audience that they would not be applicable elsewhere. They were meant for general and ongoing use in the churches. Paul's indication of a sign that he made in every letter (2 Thess 3:17; cf. Gal 6:11) was perhaps his way of helping his readers avoid letters falsely ascribed to him (2 Thess 2:2), although it has been suggested that 2 Thess 2:2 is talking about misuse of a letter like 1 Thessalonians that Paul actually wrote.[29]

---

29. In addition to Paul's letters, the letter to the Hebrews refers to itself as a "word of exhortation" (Heb 13:22), suggesting that it might be a homily of sorts (cf. Acts 13:15). 2 Peter makes some comments about scriptural texts in general that will be part of the discussion in the following chapter (2 Pet 1:19-21; 3:16). See also the references to writing in Rev 1:19; 5:1; 10:9-10 [cf. Ezek 2:8; 3:1-3]; 22:9-10, 18-19.

3

Canon Consciousness

WHILE IT IS TRUE that the use of the term "canon" is somewhat anachronistic, the conception of an authoritative and closed list of scriptural writings is not entirely foreign to the biblical texts themselves (Deut 4:2; Prov 30:6; Rev 22:18–19). But this definition of canon does not tell the whole story of why the Tanakh and the New Testament documents emerged from a larger body of religious literature without a formal decree. Stephen Chapman has suggested that what makes the biblical books "canonical" is the fact that they were shaped in light of one another and intended to be read together.[1] That is, there was an awareness of the corpus of biblical literature that went into the final formation of the texts themselves. The evidence of this canon consciousness is not only the complex web of inner-biblical exegesis and intertextuality found in the Bible but also the inner-biblical references to canonical divisions (e.g., Zech 7:12).[2] For Chapman, this primarily involves various references to "the Law and the Prophets" within the Tanakh. He argues on this basis that the Prophets have not been subordinated to the Law. He also does not think that this designation includes a distinct Writings division. Of course, the New Testament shows an awareness of this division (e.g., Luke 24:44), but it remains to be seen whether this is part of the conception within the Tanakh. It will also be of interest to explore the New Testament's consciousness of its own canonicity and its textual relationship to the Tanakh. It is often

1. Chapman, *Law and the Prophets*.

2. See Fishbane, *Biblical Interpretation*; Shepherd, *Textual World of the Bible*; Shepherd, *Text in the Middle*.

said that the biblical documents were not created in a vacuum. This is true, but what is the alternative to the vacuum? Is it a reconstructed historical context? The evidence from this chapter suggests that the alternative is a canon that provides the interpretive context and structural framework for the biblical texts. It must be stressed again, however, that it was not a post-biblical decision to read the texts this way. It was a decision that went into the very making and arranging of the books.

The Seams of the Tanakh

One way to begin this discussion is to look at the canon from the top down to see if there is any correlation between the way the Torah connects to the Prophets and the way the Prophets connect to the Writings.[3] While it was not possible to put the Tanakh on a single scroll in antiquity, it was possible to include compositional seam work in the introductions and conclusions to individual books and larger divisions that would dictate the arrangement in which the texts were to be read. The seams that connect the Torah to the Prophets (Deut 34:5—Josh 1:9) and the Prophets to the Writings (Mal 3:22 [Eng., 4:4]—Ps 1) betray the work of a composer/author.

This arrangement obviously presupposes the placement of the book of Psalms at the head of the Writings division (4QMMT; Luke 24:44; Philo *Contempl.* 1f., 25). The similarity and uniqueness of the language at these strategic junctures can hardly be coincidental. Furthermore, this seam work sends an eschatological message that had and has a global impact on the reading of the lower levels of the canon. The text commends itself as the object of study for the wise person (Deut 34:9; Josh 1:8; Ps 1:2) who waits in expectation of the messianic prophet like Moses (Deut 34:10) whose forerunner, the prophet like Elijah (Mal 3:23 [Eng., 4:5]), will prepare the way before the Day of YHWH (cf. Luke 1:17; Acts 3:22). Of particular interest here is the way in which this seam

---

3. See Blenkinsopp, *Prophecy and Canon*, 86-95, 120-23; Sailhamer, *Introduction to OT Theology*, 239-49.

work is based on exegesis of texts already present within the Torah and the Prophets (Num 27:18; Deut 18:15, 18; Mal 3:1).[4]

The appendix to Malachi (Mal 3:22-24 [Eng., 4:4-6]), which stands apart from the formulaic disputations that form the main body of the book, also makes a fitting conclusion to the Book of the Twelve whose eschatological program is set forth in Hos 3:4-5. It begins by looking back to the Torah of Moses (Mal 3:22 [Eng., 4:4]), but the LXX places this first verse of the appendix last, anticipating the reference to the Torah in Ps 1:2. The fact that Ps 1:2 is essentially a citation of Josh 1:8 is critical, indicating to the reader that the Torah here is not merely the Sinai law but the book of the Torah (i.e., the Pentateuch). Already in the introduction to the book of Psalms (Pss 1-2; see *b. Ber.* 9b-10a) there seems to be an awareness of the Torah and the Prophets as well as the book's position at the beginning of the Writings. Not only does Psalm 1 refer back to the Torah, but also Psalm 2 highlights the messianic message of the Torah and the Prophets, preparing the reader for a reading of Scripture (e.g., Pss 78; 105; 106; 136) that spans from Moses (Ps 90) to David (Pss 3-41 etc.) to the exile (e.g., Ps 137) and finally to the post-exilic period (e.g., Ps 126).[5]

The Law and the Prophets

The close relationship between the Torah and the Prophets is evident in the role assigned to the prophets in the preservation, teaching, and shaping of the Torah, not to mention the influence of the Torah on the prophetic writings. According to Deut 31:9-13, the priests were originally entrusted with the Torah, but this responsibility was not maintained as evidenced by the need for the rediscovery of the Torah by the high priest Hilkiah in the days of Josiah (2 Kgs 22:8; cf. 2 Chr 17:7-9). Who then did ensure the transmission of the Torah? According to 2 Kgs 17:13, YHWH sent

---

4. The Mal 3:1 text is itself a reading of an earlier text in Exod 23:20 (cf. Mark 1:2).

5. This feature of the book led Martin Luther to refer to the book of Psalms as a "little Bible" (*kleine Bibel*).

his Torah to the people by means of his servants the prophets (cf. Jer 25:4; 2 Chr 36:15-16). The prayers of Daniel (Dan 9:10) and Ezra (Ezra 9:10-11) reiterate that the Torah was given through the prophets. On the one hand, this makes sense because Moses himself was a prophet (Deut 18:15, 18; 34:10), and later prophets were modeled after him (e.g., Jer 1:4-10). Furthermore, the macrostructure of the Pentateuch reflects a prophetic perspective rather than a priestly one (Gen 3:14-19; 49; Exod 15; Num 23-24; Deut 32-33).[6] On the other hand, several of the prophets were priests (e.g., Jeremiah, Ezekiel, and Zechariah). This would explain their access to the texts and to the scribal training necessary for the task of reading and producing large literary works. Ezra himself, who was of priestly lineage and who had a hand in the making of the Torah (Ezra 7:6, 10), acknowledged his debt to the prophets (Ezra 9:10-11).

At the beginning of the book of Isaiah, the prophet calls on the leadership and the people to hear "the word of YHWH" and to pay attention to "the Torah of our God" (Isa 1:10). Then again in Isaiah's vision of the last days he says "Torah" will go forth from Zion and "the word of YHWH" from Jerusalem (Isa 2:3). On the surface these may appear to be general references to divine instruction. In fact, one might even argue that this is what these terms meant at an earlier oral stage. But now it is necessary to reckon with the meaning of these terms within the corpus of canonical Scripture. The phrase "the word of YHWH" is primarily used to introduce subunits within the prophetic writings of Jeremiah (82X), Ezekiel (99X), and Zechariah (18X).[7] As such it is a fitting designation for the body of prophetic writings known from elsewhere (e.g., Ezek 38:17; Zech 1:4; Dan 9:2). When coupled with the term "Torah," the likely conclusion is that the book of the Torah (Josh 1:8; Ps 1:2; Neh 8-9) and the prophetic writings (i.e.,

---

6. See Sailhamer, *Pentateuch as Narrative*, 36. See also Schmitt, "Redaktion des Pentateuch," 170-89.

7. It also occurs frequently in the Former Prophets, particularly the book of Kings (71X), to refer to the message that came from God through the prophets.

the Prophets) are in view. This in turn could provide insight into the enigmatic references to "Testimony" and "Torah" in Isa 8:16, 20. The prophet urges adherence to Moses and the Prophets in the face of temptation to seek alternative modes of revelation.[8]

The references to a known collection of prophetic writings (Ezek 38:17; Zech 1:4; 7:7, 12; Dan 9:2) all cite the book of Jeremiah in particular. This is significant for several reasons. First of all, it attests to the prominence of the book of Jeremiah among the other prophetic writings (cf. *b. B. Bat.* 14b: Jeremiah, Ezekiel, Isaiah). But it also suggests that the book of Jeremiah was not so prominent that it was cited alone and apart from the other prophetic writings. That is, the very collection of the prophetic writings was considered important enough to earn mention even when only one of the books was actually cited. No one prophetic book was greater than the Prophets.

Ezekiel refers to Jeremiah's prophecy about the enemy from the north (Jer 1:13-15; 25:1-13) in an address to Gog who is said to be coming in the last days from the remote parts of the north (Ezek 38:14-16): "Thus says YHWH, 'Are you not the one of whom I spoke in former days by the hand of my servants the prophets of Israel who prophesied in those days, years, to bring you upon them'" (Ezek 38:17)? Ezekiel follows the first edition of Jeremiah as represented by the LXX and 4QJer[b, d], which does not identify the enemy from the north with Babylon as does the MT. This is also true of the reading of Jeremiah in Daniel 9. According to Dan 9:2, Daniel was reading about Jeremiah's prophecy of seventy years (Jer 25:11; 29:10) in the "books" (*sefarim*) in the first year of Darius (cf. 2 Chr 36:20-23). Daniel took this to be a

---

8. Binding and sealing (Isa 8:16) are actions performed with written documents (e.g., Dan 12:4). The term "Testimony," which only occurs here and in Ruth 4:7, is generally taken to be the prophetic witness (BDB, 730), but "Torah" would not ordinarily be a word for written prophetic instruction. The book of the Torah is the book of Moses. The action of sealing the documents is normally understood to be preservation of them until the time of the fulfillment of their prophecies. But the context suggests that the texts were also to be read in the meantime in order to engender hope in the future. Thus, the prophet says, "To Torah and to Testimony" (Isa 8:20).

prophecy about seventy literal years in Babylonian captivity (Jer 29:10), but the angel Gabriel came along and pushed the prophecy into the indefinite future—"seventy sevens" (Dan 9:24–27). This understanding of the prophecy is only an exegetical possibility if the text of Jer 25:1–13 is the one behind the LXX.[9] That text does not explicitly mention the Babylonian captivity, leaving the number "seventy" open to an interpretation in which it stands for a complete, indefinite period of time.

Zechariah mentions "the former prophets" (*hanneviim harishonim*) three times (Zech 1:4; 7:7, 12), the only three times in the entire Hebrew Bible. The context of the first mention in Zech 1:4 suggests that these were the pre-exilic prophets like Jeremiah and Ezekiel who warned about impending judgment but were ignored. From the vantage point of Zechariah's time the people could see that the words of those prophecies were true, so they would do well to listen to the prophets in their own day. Furthermore, those words were now directly accessible in written form. The citation in Zech 1:4 most closely matches the text of Jer 23:22; 25:5–7. Thus, Zechariah finds himself in the role of an exegete interpreting the texts of the prophets as a prophet. This function of the prophet is reflected in the LXX of Prov 29:18. The MT of this text simply reads, "Without prophetic vision (*chazon*) a people is let loose, but as for one who keeps Torah, happy is he." The LXX interprets *chazon* ("prophetic vision") to be an *exegetes* ("exegete"). That is, the prophetic vision stands by metonymy for the prophet himself who is not only one who receives visions and dreams but also one who reads and interprets the text of Scripture—both the Torah and the Prophets—which is why prophetic vision is parallel to keeping Torah.[10] It also explains why the very fabric of biblical composition is made of inner-biblical exegesis and intertextuality. The text of

---

9. See Shepherd, *Daniel in the Context*, 39, 95–99.

10. Note also this role of the prophet in 1 Corinthians 14 where prophecy is grouped with revelation, knowledge, and teaching (1 Cor 14:6) in contrast to tongues lacking interpretation (1 Cor 14:5). Prophecy is what edifies the church (1 Cor 14:3, 12, 19, 22, 24). The description of prophecy in 1 Cor 14:3 most closely matches Paul's instruction to Timothy to devote himself to the reading and teaching of Scripture (1 Tim 4:13).

Zech 7:12 refers to "the Torah and the words that YHWH of hosts sent by his Spirit by the hand of the former prophets." This is different from the giving of the Torah through the prophets (2 Kgs 17:13; Dan 9:10; Ezra 9:10-11). Here the conjunction *waw* ("and") coordinates two distinct entities: (1) the Torah and (2) the words of the prophets. The text also highlights the role of the Spirit not only in the prophets themselves (Num 11:29; Mic 2:8) but also in the making of their books (2 Tim 3:16; 2 Pet 1:19-21).

The Law and the Prophets and the Writings

Apart from the canonical seams, there is perhaps no greater piece of evidence internal to the Tanakh for the threefold shape of the canon than the placement of the book of Chronicles at its conclusion (Matt 23:35; *b. B. Bat.* 14b). This book begins with Adam (1 Chr 1:1), works its way through the narrative of the Torah and the Former Prophets, and concludes with an abbreviated version of the decree of Cyrus (2 Chr 36:22-23) from Ezra 1:1-4, presupposing a canon before it that consists of Moses, the Prophets, and the Writings (ending w/Ezra-Nehemiah and Chronicles). Along the way the Chronicler shows his familiarity with the prophetic book of Isaiah (2 Chr 32:32) as well as the book of Psalms (e.g., 1 Chr 16:8-36 // Pss 96; 105:1-15; 106:47-48).

The threefold shape of the canon is also attested in a variety of early sources outside of the Tanakh (e.g., the prologue to Sirach; 4QMMT; Luke 24:44; Philo, *Contempl.* 1f., 25),[11] but more recently there has been some debate about the third division designated by these sources. For example, the prologue to Sirach simply refers to the third division as "the others." For many, this indicates uncertainty about what books occupied this division and about whether or not the third division was closed. On the other hand, such a

---

11. The placement of the Prophets last as attested by Codex Vaticanus became dominant in the Greek and Latin traditions of the Christian church, but this arrangement is unknown in Hebrew tradition, and the prologue to Sirach would seem to suggest that this was also not the original arrangement of the Greek canon.

designation as "the others" might indicate the exact opposite. For instance, if a professor enters a classroom and instructs the class to take out their "textbooks," he/she is working under the assumption that the class knows exactly what their textbooks are. If he/she has to call out the authors and titles by name, then the assumption is that the class does not yet know the corpus of literature designated by "textbooks." Likewise, the designation "the others" may in fact presuppose that readers knew precisely what books occupied the third division and did not have to be told. A simple comparison of Luke 24:44 (cf. 4QMMT) and Philo suggests that the third division began with Psalms and also included other books. Although Hebrew tradition shows some minor variation in the arrangement of this third division, the internal composition of the Writings has ensured the stability of the books that have occupied it from the beginning.

The New Testament documents, in continuity with other early sources such as the Dead Sea Scrolls, refer to the entirety of the Tanakh using a range of terminology: e.g., "the Scriptures" (1 Cor 15:3-4; cf. 2 Tim 3:15; 4:13), "the Law" (*nomos* = Torah; John 10:34; Rom 3:19), "the prophetic writings" (Rom 1:2; 16:26), "the Law and the Prophets" (Matt 5:17; Luke 24:27; Rom 3:21), "the Law of Moses and the Prophets and Psalms" (Luke 24:44), etc. There has been a recent tendency to isolate "the Law and the Prophets" from this list and to argue that the canon had only a twofold shape that either included or excluded all or part of the books of the Writings. But this misses the use and the interrelationship of the terminology.[12] The phrase "the Law and the Prophets" in Luke 24:27 clearly refers to the same body of writings as "the Law of Moses and the Prophets and Psalms" in Luke 24:44 without saying anything about how many divisions are in the canon.[13] Likewise, the designations "the Law" and "the prophetic writings" do not indicate a canon without any division. The individual terms can

---

12. See Chapman, *Law and the Prophets*, 276-79.

13. The fact that this use of "the Law and the Prophets" to refer to the Tanakh obviously assumes a precedent raises the question of whether or not designations like Zech 7:12 already refer to the threefold canon.

be used to refer either to a division or the whole depending on the context. When the terms are combined, their individual scope is limited according to whether the combination is of two or three.

The New Testament authors stand in a firm exegetical relationship to the Tanakh and do not understand their documents to be part of the threefold structure of the Hebrew canon (1 Cor 4:6).[14] They do, however, show an awareness of their own canon formation. Thus, Paul can cite Deut 25:4 as Scripture alongside Matt 10:10; Luke 10:7 (1 Tim 5:18; cf. 1 Cor 9:9). Peter compares a corpus of Pauline letters to the Hebrew Scriptures (2 Pet 3:16). This status for the New Testament documents likely comes from statements like John 14:26 (cf. *Jub.* 32:24–25; 2 Tim 3:16; 2 Pet 1:19–21). There even seems to be intent behind the arrangement of some of these documents. The division of Luke-Acts is certainly no accident, and the placement of John between the two volumes (particularly John 14–16) is a fitting interlude between the expectation of the Spirit at the end of Luke and the coming of the Spirit at the beginning of Acts. Surely what is said at the end of the New Testament in Rev 22:18–19 can be called canon conscious.

Reading in the Context of the Canon

Chapman's treatment of the Law and the Prophets includes a discussion of extra-biblical literature like the Dead Sea Scrolls, the Apocrypha, and the Pseudepigrapha.[15] One body of literature he does not include, however, is that of the Targums. It is well known that the Targums incorporate material from across the canon of Hebrew Scriptures in their interpretive renderings of biblical books. But the presence of these renderings in the wisdom literature is unique due to the fact that references to biblical narratives such as those in Genesis–Kings, while somewhat common in the Hebrew books of the Prophets and Psalms, are relatively sparse in books

---

14. See Seitz, "Two Testaments and the Failure," 195–211.
15. Chapman, *Law and the Prophets*, 241–75.

Canon Consciousness

like Job, Proverbs, and Ecclesiastes.[16] Apart from the occasional mention of Solomon (e.g., Prov 1:1; 10:1; 25:1), there appears on the surface to be little that connects this literature to the rest of the canon. While this is not entirely the case, biblical theologians have historically struggled to locate this segment of the Hebrew Bible within their overall conception of the Bible's theology. The Targums, on the other hand, have little difficulty in reading the wisdom literature within the context of the canon. Furthermore, what prompts their renderings is often fairly obvious from the Hebrew text. Sometimes these renderings are what might be called fanciful, but there are many places where the Targums can help the reader see real links in the original text to other biblical books, resulting in a reading of the text that is not so isolated.

The book of Job has more connections to the larger canon than one might think at first glance. Not only is Job's God YHWH (Job 1:21), the God of the patriarchs, but also Job is cast as an Abraham-like character: Job 1:1, 3, 5; 42:6, 8, 17 (cf. Gen 12:7-8, 16; 17:1; 18:27; 20:7; 25:8; *b. B. Bat.* 15b-16b). The book shares with the Pentateuch the goal of teaching the fear of YHWH (Deut 31:13; Job 28:28; cf. Prov 1:7; 9:10; Eccl 12:13). Its hymnic material is comparable to that found in the Prophets and Psalms (e.g., Job 5:9-13; 9:5-10; 12:13-25). But the Targum of Job goes well beyond this to include the following in its rendering: Dinah (Job 2:9; see Gen 34; *Gen. Rab.* 73:9; *b. B. Bat.* 15a); Jeremiah and Jonah (Job 3:6); Torah (Job 3:16; 5:7; 11:8; 24:13; 30:4; 36:33; 37:21); Abraham, Isaac, and Jacob (Job 3:19; 15:10); the generation of the Flood (Job 4:8; 6:17; 22:7; 24:2); Esau and Ishmael (Job 4:10-11; 15:19-20); the Egyptians and the wise men of Pharaoh (Job 5:12-13); Abraham alone (Job 5:17; 30:19; 32:2); Balaam (Job 5:21); Sihon and Og (Job 5:22); the Sanctuary (Job 5:24; 23:13); the drowning of the Egyptians and Pharaoh (Job 7:12; 38:23); the sons of Ishmael, the Ammonites, the Moabites, and Pharaoh (Job 12:6); Moses' exodus and Joshua's exodus (Job 14:11); Lot and Abraham (Job

---

16. On the other hand, the presence of wisdom features across the canon is quite noticeable (e.g., Deut 4:6; Hos 14:10 [Eng., 14:9]; Ps 1). See Childs, *Biblical Theology*, 187-90.

14:18); Korah, Dathan, and Abiram (Job 15:29; see Num 16); Noah (Job 22:19); Michael and Gabriel (Job 25:2); the Garden of Eden, the tree of life, Adam, and the serpent (Job 28:6–8; 38:18); Israel (Job 28:22; 38:13); the sons of Aaron (Job 37:1). Perhaps the most insightful of these are the reference to Jeremiah in Job 3:6 and the reference to the exodus in Job 14:11. The specific wording of Job's lament in chapter 3 is most closely matched by Jeremiah's confession in Jer 20:14–18. And the correlation between Moses' exodus (Exod 14:21–22) and the new exodus led by the new Moses, Joshua (Josh 3), is one established by the wording of the biblical text itself.

In contrast to the Targum of Job, the Targum of Proverbs makes very little reference to Moses and the Prophets apart from the mention of prophecy in Prov 30:1; 31:1. This is perhaps because the Hebrew book has already made the connection to Solomon (Prov 1:1; 10:1; 25:1), setting the collection of proverbial sayings firmly within the context of the story of the divine gift of wisdom to Solomon (1 Kgs 3; 5:9–14 [Eng., 4:29–34]; cf. Prov 2:6). The Targum of Ecclesiastes, on the other hand, is completely saturated with such reference, resulting in a rendering that overwhelms the original text. References to the Torah are the most common,[17] but due to the fact that Qoheleth is a Solomon-like figure, not to mention the Jewish traditions about Solomon, references to Solomon are also frequent.[18] Other references include the following: the Messiah (Eccl 1:11; 7:24); Eden (Eccl 1:15; 9:7); Saul (Eccl 2:15); Rehoboam and Jeroboam (Eccl 2:18; 3:11; 4:15–16; 10:16); Abraham and Nimrod (Eccl 4:13–14; 7:28); Adam (Eccl 6:10; 7:28–29); the Temple (Eccl 7:4); Joseph and his brothers (Eccl 7:19); the Tower of Babel (Eccl 7:28); the prophets (Eccl 8:1); Manasseh (Eccl 10:9); the fiery serpents (Eccl 10:11; see Num 21); Hezekiah (Eccl 10:17); Moses (Eccl 12:10–11). Interest in the Torah is common to the Targums in general, but there is usually something in the original text that gives rise to mention of the Torah in the rendering. In the case of the wisdom literature, Torah is wisdom (Deut

---

17. Eccl 1:3, 15; 2:10, 25; 3:12; 4:17; 5:11, 17; 6:5–6, 8, 12; 7:5, 7, 11–12, 17–18, 23; 8:15–16; 9:1, 4; 10:2, 4, 9, 11, 17–18; 11:7–8; 12:10, 12.

18. Eccl 1:1–2, 4, 12–13; 3:11–12; 4:15; 7:27; 9:7, 11, 13; 10:7, 9; 12:8–10.

4:6; Sir 24). Furthermore, the Hebrew text of Ecclesiastes already features verbal links to the text of the Torah (e.g., Gen 3:19; Eccl 3:20). And finally, Qoheleth (Solomon) is a king entrusted with the responsibility of the Torah (Deut 17:14–20; 1 Kgs 2:3). While the reader may ultimately disagree with the Jewish tradition about the end of Solomon's life imposed on the text (Eccl 1:1–2), he or she can still appreciate the attempt to wrestle with the text in the context of the canon (Eccl 1:12, 16).[19]

---

19. For further reading on canon consciousness, see Spellman, *Toward a Canon-Conscious*.

4

Torah lishma

> We have been studying cheerfully and seriously. As far as I was concerned it could have continued in that way, and I had already resigned myself to having my grave here by the Rhine! I had plans for the future with other colleagues who are either no longer here or have been away for a long time—but there has been a frost on our spring night! And now the end has come. So listen to my last piece of advice: exegesis, exegesis and yet more exegesis! Keep to the Word, to the scripture that has been given us.[1]

COMPARABLE LAST WORDS OCCUR in Paul's final letter (2 Tim 3:10—4:8) accompanied by a request for "the books, especially the parchments" (2 Tim 4:13). For many, this kind of devotion to Scripture in such dire circumstances might seem impractical, but these men understood that God's revelation of himself in a book in many ways means that exegesis is life. Furthermore, this exegesis is not a matter of using the Bible to address issues of importance to the reader. It is a giving over of oneself to the terms and conditions of the text. The specific form and sequence of the biblical books dictates everything so that the Bible is read for its own sake. The Jewish rabbis have a phrase for this kind of reading: *torah lishma* ("Torah for its own sake"):[2]

---

1. Karl Barth's farewell to his students in Bonn prior to his expulsion from Nazi Germany in 1935. Quoted in Busch, *Karl Barth*, 259.

2. "In the view of the rabbis, God and the Torah were intimately linked to one another, and for them studying the Torah was a way of communicating with God. Accordingly, studying for its own sake (*torah lishma*) is considered far more important than the outcome of the interpretation of individual legal

Torah lishma

Rabbi Meir said: Anyone who engages in Torah study for its own sake (*lishma*) merits many things. Not only that, but the entire world is worthwhile for him alone. He is called "friend" and "beloved," he loves G-d, he loves man, he brings joy to G-d, he brings joy to man. It [the Torah] clothes him in humility and fear. It enables him to be righteous, pious, upright, and faithful. It distances him from sin and brings him to merit. [Others] benefit from him advice and wisdom, understanding and strength, as it says, "To me is advice and wisdom, I am understanding, and strength is mine" (Prov 8:14). It gives him kingship, dominion, and analytical judgment. It reveals to him the secrets of the Torah. He becomes as an increasing stream and an unceasing river. He becomes modest, slow to anger, and forgiving of the wrongs done to him. It makes him great and exalted above all of creation (Pirkei Avos Ch. 6).

This quote from Rabbi Meir does not explain *torah lishma*.[3] It assumes that its meaning is self-evident and goes on to celebrate the virtues of those who study the Torah for its own sake.[4] Those who engage in this kind of Torah study stand in right relationship to God and far from sin (cf. Ps 19). Because they remain close to the source of wisdom, they also benefit those who are around them (cf. Ps 1).

---

cases or verses. After the destruction of the temple, the Torah became the most important sign of the continued existence of the covenantal relationship between God and Israel, and the study of Torah became the principal way of preserving that relationship. Biblical interpretation became, in David Stern's words, 'a kind of conversation the Rabbis invented in order to enable God to speak to them from between the lines of Scripture . . . [t]he multiplication of interpretations in midrash was a way, as it were, to prolong that conversation'" (Zetterholm, *Jewish Interpretation*, 36).

3. Cf. *b. Ber.* 17a; *b. Pesah.* 50b; *b. Arak.* 16b; *b. Sotah* 47a; *b. Naz.* 23b; *b. Hor.* 10b; *b. Hul.* 30a; *b. Sukkah* 49b; *b. Taan.* 7a; *b. Sanh.* 26b; 99b.

4. "It is difficult to overestimate the importance attached by Pharisaic-Rabbinic Judaism to the *study of the Torah*. In fact, a classic, ongoing controversy centered about whether the study of the *Torah* or the fulfilling of the *Torah* was more important" (Levine, *Aramaic Version of the Bible*, 137). See *b. Qidd.* 40b.

How might the church and the academy implement the study of Scripture for its own sake? For the church, it is important to recognize that the task of interpretation is not to contextualize the Bible. It is to contextualize the reader.[5] The constant rush to make the Bible applicable too often runs against the grain of what the biblical authors are developing and fails to trust that the biblical texts are applicable the way they are (2 Tim 3:15–17) if their readers will only have the patience to wait on them. The biblical authors intend their books to be read by future generations (e.g., Deut 31:9–13) and by multiple audiences (e.g., Col 4:6), so it is imperative for modern readers not to bypass this function of the texts themselves in favor of generating a separate update of what they read.

For the academy, efforts to discover what is behind the text must at least be equaled by efforts to see the text itself. Institutions of higher education that claim to have a high view of Scripture often do not back this up in their curricula. Where are the courses of study on textual criticism? Why do we not require elementary, intermediate, and advanced Hebrew and Greek? Why do we not require biblical Aramaic? Why are our book study courses in English rather than in the original languages? Where are the courses on the Septuagint and the Targums? Instead we favor courses in theology and "practical" ministry that simply talk around the Bible. If the answer to these questions has something to do with marketability and competition with other institutions, then it is time to ask why it is that we do what we do.[6]

The following discussion offers two examples of the kind of Bible study that is generally absent in the church and in seminaries. First, literary analysis of certain features of biblical narrative (e.g., setting, plot, characterization, etc.) is something that the

---

5. "It is important to note the direction of interpretation. Typology does not make scriptural contents into metaphors for extrascriptural realities, but the other way around. It does not suggest, as is often said in our day, that believers find their stories in the Bible, but rather that they make the story of the Bible their story" (Lindbeck, *Nature of Doctrine*, 118).

6. That is, do we want jacks of all trades and masters of none, or do we want masters of what is most important?

average reader of an English Bible in the church can do without prior knowledge of the biblical languages. Too often interpretation of narrative is done in a kind of *ad hoc* fashion without any real understanding of the techniques that are available to writers when communicating through the medium of storytelling (and how to identify them). Second, the convergence of biblical language study, textual analysis, and compositional analysis is something that is generally missing in the preparation of those who plan to teach the Bible in the local church or in higher education. An example of such a study is offered here.

Character Study: Depersonalization of Antagonists in the Hebrew Bible

One of the great gains in literary study of the Bible has been the growing awareness of storytelling techniques and in particular the many ways in which writers depict and present their characters to their readers.[7] Interpreters now look for the role a character plays (major or minor), the extent of his/her development (round or flat), and the character's virtue (good, bad, or somewhere in between). It is well known that authors will often employ their major protagonist as their mouthpiece to communicate their own message (e.g., Gen 45:7; 50:20) given the fact that storytellers typically do not speak directly to their audiences. Some of the best and most interesting characters are those like David who are fully developed in major protagonist roles with good virtue and yet with a major flaw. In addition to such considerations as these, the viewpoint from which the story is told is critical to the reader's perspective. Readers tend to sympathize with characters from whose vantage point the story is written, almost without regard to the character's virtue.[8] On the other hand, writers can create con-

---

7. See Alter, *Art of Biblical Narrative*, 143–62; Bar-Efrat, *Narrative Art in the Bible*, 47–92; Berlin, *Poetics and Interpretation*, 23–42; Fokkelman, *Reading Biblical Narrative*, 55–72; Sternberg, *Poetics of Biblical Narrative*, 342–64.

8. Sometimes a character wins the favor of readers on the basis of their outward appearance. For example, readers typically view Rachel in a positive

siderable distance between readers and characters they want to be viewed negatively. The present section is devoted to the technique of depersonalizing antagonists in an effort to avoid any sympathy that might be directed toward them, making it easy for readers to celebrate their downfall.

The Joseph story (Gen 37–50) provides an initial example from the perspective of his brothers. Of course, Joseph is an exemplary and virtually flawless character as far as the reader is concerned, yet this is exactly what makes his relationship with his brothers so dynamic. The story begins with an account of their jealousy toward Joseph and their attempt to rid themselves of him (Gen 37). When Joseph and his brothers meet again in Egypt, he recognizes them, but they do not recognize him (Gen 42:7–8). Joseph uses this to his advantage and deals harshly with his brothers. Henceforth the brothers refer to Joseph not by name or by title but as "the man" (e.g., Gen 43:3). This depersonalization of Joseph's character shows that from their vantage point Joseph is simply a difficult ruler who is unnecessarily and confusingly unhelpful—someone with whom the brothers do not connect at all. The fact that Joseph is actually their brother seeking to reengage them creates suspense for the reader as he or she watches the story unfold, leading up to the climactic revelation of Joseph's identity in chapter 45.[9]

Another example would be the way in which enemies of the people of God are portrayed. The exodus story (Exod 1–19), for instance, never mentions the Pharaoh by name. This is in stark contrast to the way rulers of foreign enemies are often depicted (e.g., Nebuchadnezzar), but the depersonalization of the Pharaoh

---

light, yet there is little in the description of her virtue that commends her. Her beauty, however, reminds readers of other characters whose good appearance is a reflection of their inner virtue. A modern analogy might be the character played by Paul Newman in the 1963 film *Hud*. Newman's character had all the external graces but lacked inner beauty. Nevertheless, audiences loved him. A more complex biblical example would be Absalom, an undoubtedly winsome character with whom readers could certainly sympathize in the wake of the Amnon and Tamar incident, yet in the end he was a tragic character.

9. See Sternberg, *Poetics of Biblical Narrative*, 285–308.

makes it easier for the reader to accept the divine hardening of his heart and his ultimate downfall. A unique occurrence of this sort of technique is in the David and Goliath story (1 Sam 17–18). Goliath is introduced by name (1 Sam 17:4), but with the exception of 1 Sam 17:23 (> LXX), he is only known as "the Philistine" for the remainder of the story (e.g., 1 Sam 17:10). On the one hand, this highlights Goliath's role as the representative of the Philistines, but it also distances the reader from Goliath and makes it nearly impossible for the reader to sympathize with him in any way. On the other hand, David is known by name throughout the narrative, and it is clearly the author's intention to have the reader identify closely with David. Depersonalization of foreign enemies also has eschatological implications. The description of Gog (Ezek 38–39), while closely associated with lands known from Gen 10:2–5, does not match any known historical ruler or nation. He is simply the unidentified "enemy from the north" who will appear in the last days (Ezek 38:14–17; cf. Jer 1:13–15; 25:1–13 LXX; Num 24:7 LXX; Rev 20:8).

One last example involves a slightly different use of depersonalization. Several messianic prophecies simply refer to a figure as the "man" (Num 24:7, 17 LXX; Isa 19:20 LXX; Zech 6:12; cf. John 19:5; 1 Tim 2:5). This creates a sense of mystery about the historical identity of this figure—something that the Gospel of John seeks to rectify (John 20:30–31). But even this relatively innocuous use of depersonalization can turn negative in the hands of those who oppose the man. In John 7:11, the Jewish leaders refer to Jesus as "that one" and again in John 11:47 as "this man," refusing to grant him any respect whatsoever.[10]

---

10. This calls to mind the presidential debate between John McCain and Barack Obama in which McCain consistently referred to Obama as "that one"—an incredibly disrespectful gesture that did not go over very well with viewers.

A Textual Study: The Written Source of the MT-only Version of 1 Samuel 17–18

The corrupt nature of the traditional Hebrew text (MT) of the book of Samuel is well known.[11] The major differences between this text and the LXX of Samuel, which is a mixture of the Old Greek translation and proto/*kaige*-Theodotion, have also been recognized.[12] Furthermore, the discovery of the Dead Sea Scrolls has revealed a Hebrew text of Samuel—in particular 4QSam^a—that differs considerably from the MT and at times agrees with the LXX against the MT.[13] In addition to the numerous small-scale variations among these witnesses, there are several large-scale literary variants:[14] (1) the MT, LXX, and 4QSam^a bear witness to three different editions of the Song of Hannah (1 Sam 2:1–10) and its placement relative to the story of Samuel's birth and presentation at the sanctuary; (2) 4QSam^a features a longer text of 1 Samuel 11 than that of the MT and LXX; and (3) there are two editions of the story of David and Goliath (1 Sam 17–18) in the LXX (the shorter edition) and the MT (the longer edition).

Emanuel Tov has provided an invaluable contribution to the study of the last of the aforementioned examples (1 Sam 17–18).[15] According to Tov, the LXX and the MT represent two different Hebrew editions of 1 Samuel 17–18. That is, the LXX translator

---

11. See Driver, *Notes on the Hebrew Text*.

12. Thackeray, *Septuagint and Jewish Worship*, 9–28; Barthélemy, *Les Devanciers d'Aquila*, 34–41. (Proto-)Lucian partly supplies the Old Greek for the *kaige* sections. For the possibility that medieval Hebrew variants also help with this task in the book of Kings, see Trebolle and Torijano, "Behavior of the Hebrew Medieval Manuscripts," 101–33.

13. MT-Chronicles and the Greek text employed by Josephus for *The Jewish Antiquities* also bear significant similarity to 4QSam^a (see Ulrich, *Dead Sea Scrolls*, 184–201).

14. See Tov, *Textual Criticism*, 301–4, 311–13; Tov, *Greek and Hebrew Bible*, 333–62, 433–55. This situation is generally consistent with the presence of variant literary editions throughout the corpus of biblical Hebrew literature (see Ulrich, *Dead Sea Scrolls*, 3–120).

15. Tov, *Greek and Hebrew Bible*, 333–62.

did not significantly alter a Hebrew source that was more or less identical to the MT. Rather, the *Vorlage* was a shorter and earlier version of the David and Goliath story. Tov also argues that the LXX and the MT-only sections each constitute independent accounts of the narrative. The MT-only story, which may have once existed in fuller form, was inserted into the LXX version of the story, creating a longer and later edition. Thus, the LXX version did not simply grow on its own. It was supplemented by the already independent MT-only account.

For Tov, this raises several important questions. If the LXX version is literarily prior to the MT-only version, does that also mean that it is more original in terms of the history of the tradition? Also, given the alleged inconsistencies that the conflated version creates, why was the MT-only version only preserved in the form of the longer, later edition now known in the MT? Tov assumes that the MT-only version was derived from a written source, but does not go into any detail about what that written source may have looked like or what may have been the basis for it. Is there any way to make any further comment from the available evidence?

The present section essentially agrees with the foundation laid by Tov and attempts to pursue the remaining questions at the conclusion of his essay. In particular, it sets forth the thesis that the Hebrew text behind the LXX was the written source for the MT-only account, which was intended to be a short summary of the story. This can be demonstrated by showing that the thematic and terminological materials of the LXX version formed the very fabric of the MT-only story and that the direction of dependence could not have been the other way. This would also solve the problem of priority in the history of tradition. As for the question of the manner in which the MT-only version was preserved, it will first be necessary to show that the discrepancies between the two versions are only apparent. Then it will be clear that the only way to guarantee the preservation of the story's summary was to find a way to include it within the textual transmission of the book of Samuel.

Emanuel Tov: "The Composition of 1 Samuel 16–18 in Light of the Septuagint"

Tov divides the history of scholarship on the origin of LXX 1 Samuel 16–18 into two groups: (1) those who ascribe the shorter version to the work of the Greek translator[16] and (2) those who argue that the LXX was based on a shorter Hebrew text.[17] He notes that those who fall into the first group wrote before the discovery of the Qumran scrolls and did not have the advantage of Hebrew texts that differ from the MT to the same degree that the LXX sometimes does. For his own part, Tov outlines the following methodology:

> If the translator omitted 44 percent of the text, he must have approached that text freely, and this free approach should also be visible in other details. If, on the other hand, there are indications that the translation is literal, that the translator approached the source text with care and introduced but little exegesis of his own, it is not likely that he would have omitted large sections because of exegetical (e.g., harmonistic) motives; in that case, the short text of the LXX would more likely reflect a short Hebrew text.

He examines the translation technique of 1 Samuel 17–18 in seven different areas: (1) Linguistic versus exegetical rendering, (2) Word order, (3) Quantitative representation, (4) Consistency in translation equivalents, (5) Internal consistency, (6) Adherence to the general vocabulary of the LXX, and (7) Hebraisms in the translation. This analysis shows that the translator was relatively faithful to his Hebrew source and would not have been likely to make

---

16. Kuenen, *Historisch-kritische Einleitung*, I, 2, 61; Budde, *Bücher Richter und Samuel*, 212; Schmid, *Septuagintageschichtliche Studien*, 118; Barthélemy, "Qualité du Texte Massorétique de Samuel," 1–44.

17. Thenius, *Bücher Samuels*, 67; Peters, *Beiträge zur Text*, 30–62; Wellhausen, *Composition des Hexateuchs*, 247; Smith, *Critical and Exegetical Commentary*, 150; Steuernagel, *Lehrbuch der Einleitung*, 317; Habel, *Literary Criticism of the OT*, 10–11; Woods, "Light Shown by the Septuagint," 21–38; Stoebe, "Goliathperikope 1 Sam. XVII.1—XVIII.5," 397–413; Johnson, *Hexaplarische Rezension*, 118–23; McCarter, *1 Samuel*.

large-scale changes on his own. Tov also suggests that Hebrew scrolls of Samuel from Qumran that contain readings previously constructed from the LXX enhance confidence in this conclusion.

Tov then addresses two passages in the MT-only material that supposedly gave rise to the translator's abridgement of his Hebrew source. In 1 Sam 17:55-58, it appears on the surface that Saul is ignorant of David despite the description of David's relationship to him in 1 Sam 16:17-23 and the discussion between the two in 1 Sam 17:31-39. Presumably the translator omitted 1 Sam 17:55-58 to avoid contradiction. Likewise, 1 Sam 18:17-19 narrates Saul's offer of his daughter Merab to David, while 1 Sam 18:20-26 tells about David's marriage to Saul's daughter Michal. Despite the deliberate effort to join the two in 1 Sam 18:21b (MT), it is argued that the translator simply removed the difficulty by omitting 1 Sam 18:17-19. To these two examples might be added 1 Sam 17:12, which seems to presuppose that the reader has not already been introduced to David in chapter 16, and 1 Sam 17:12-31 in general, which explains how David arrived at the battle scene when in fact no explanation is necessary given the fact that the reader would have assumed his presence there as Saul's armor bearer (1 Sam 16:21; see also 1 Sam 18:5, 13).

Tov responds to these examples by saying that it is highly unlikely that the translator allowed himself such liberties and acted as a sophisticated, critical scholar. Furthermore, he points out that the translator left intact other apparent difficulties in the text that he could have omitted.[18] Not only that, but also why would the translator have omitted such a large swath of material when only a small portion of that material created problems? Of course, it

18. Tov gives 1 Sam 17:33 as an example of such a difficulty, as if David were designated an unqualified warrior (in contradiction to 1 Sam 16:18) in contrast to the qualifications of Goliath. But actually the difference between the two has nothing to do with their ability to fight. It is about their age and experience. It is worth noting, however, that when David gives his credentials to fight Goliath he references his experience as a shepherd rather than his reputation as a warrior (1 Sam 17:34-37). Tov also observes other so-called doublets in Samuel that have been left unaltered by the translator(s): 1 Sam 8:1-22; 10:17-27 // 9:1—10:16; 1 Sam 19:11-17 // 19:18-24 // 20:1-42; 1 Sam 24 // 1 Sam 26. See also 1 Sam 18:10-11; 19:9-10.

is also valid to ask whether the above examples are genuinely instances of contradiction. Thus, the question in 1 Sam 17:55–58 is not about David's identity but about the name of his father. And although this information was given in 1 Sam 16:18, the king would have had no reason to remember the name of the father of one of his court servants or armor bearers. It was only when David took center stage after the defeat of Goliath that this information became important to Saul. Likewise, there is nothing contradictory about 1 Sam 18:17–19 and 1 Sam 18:20–26. Verse 19 clearly indicates that Saul simply did not fulfill his promise, paving the way for Michal. The same can be said for 1 Sam 17:12–31. Verse 12 might seem odd given the information already provided in chapter 16, but this does not make it contradictory. The reader might have expected David to be present at the scene as Saul's armor bearer, but there is nothing contradictory about David going back and forth between his father and Saul (1 Sam 17:15).

Assuming that the LXX reflects an early stage of 1 Samuel 17–18 and that the long version in the MT represents a later stage, Tov then sets forth the additional material in the long version of the story, which is parallel to the short version, as an entirely separate version of the story:

	Version 1 (LXX and MT)	Version 2 (MT only)
16:17–23	David is introduced to Saul as a skillful harper and he is made his armor bearer.	
17:1–11	Attack by the Philistines. Goliath suggests a duel with one of the Israelites.	
17:12–31		David is sent by his father to bring food to his brothers at the front. He hears Goliath and desires to meet him in a duel.

	Version 1 (LXX and MT)	Version 2 (MT only)
17:32–39	David volunteers to fight with Goliath.	
17:40–54	The duel. After Goliath's miraculous fall, the Philistines flee.	Short account of the duel (vv. 41, 48b, 50)
17:55–58		Saul asks who David is. David is introduced to Saul by Abner.
18:1–4		David and Jonathan make a covenant.
18:5–6a		David is appointed as an officer in Saul's army.
18:6b–9	Saul's jealousy of David.	
18:10–11		Saul attempts in vain to kill David.
18:12–16	David's successes.	
18:17–19		Saul offers David his eldest daughter, Merab.
18:20–27	Saul offers David his daughter Michal.	
18:29b–30		Saul's enmity for David. David's successes.

Tov says that version 1 is "a continuous and internally consistent story," noting that 1 Sam 17:32 links immediately with 1 Sam 17:11, not with 1 Sam 17:31. Version 1 lacks nothing from version 2 that is essential to its coherence. Since version 1 presupposes that it is a continuation of the story in 1 Samuel 16, and since version 2 does not (1 Sam 17:12), version 2 is a secondary addition/insertion to version 1. Furthermore, version 1 is not likely to have derived from version 2 due to the fact it would have required an overly complex process of distributing the details of the short account over the course of the several chapters in which the story now occurs.[19] While growth from smaller complexes of tradition into larger ones seems logical, the tracing of the actual textual evidence often suggests the opposite process—a tendency to summarize.[20]

For Tov, the conflation of the two versions contains a number of inconsistencies, some of which have already been addressed. Others will be addressed in the course of the following analysis. Tov also notes several attempts by the redactor to smooth out some of the difficulties (1 Sam 17:12, 15; 18:21b).[21] As indicated above, Tov believes that version 2 derived from a written source and was preserved presumably because the redactor liked certain aspects of the story that version 1 lacked. The following discussion suggests that the written source was in fact version 1. The awkward insertion of version 2 was not designed to compete with version 1. Version 2 was intended to be a separate summary of version 1, but when it became apparent that this summary would not survive on its own, it was added to the text of the book of Samuel in the sheer interest of preservation.

---

19. Tov wonders whether the tradition about David the harper and the armor bearer in version 1 is more original than the tradition about David the shepherd in version 2, but this is not really an issue when one considers the fact that the larger text of which version 1 is a part is aware of both traditions (1 Sam 16:11, 19).

20. A classic example of this is Gerhard von Rad's assessment of Deut 26:5–9, which he assumed was exactly the kind of kernel from which the traditions of the Pentateuch grew. But this does not take seriously Deuteronomy's own presentation of itself as an exposition of the Torah (Deut 1:5). See Shepherd, *Textual World of the Bible*, 25–28. "It is impossible to isolate an actual ancient credo from these, or to say whether short credal statements preceded developed narrative or are—as indeed they seem—summaries of the latter. The fact that they are all tailored to their contexts suggests the latter" (McConville, *Deuteronomy*, 379).

21. See Tov's appendices for full lists of pluses, minuses, and variant readings in the LXX.

Torah lishma

Analysis of the MT-only Version

1 Samuel 17:12–31	Source Material
ודוד בן איש אפרתי הזה מבית לחם יהודה ושמו ישי ולו שמנה בנים (v. 12a)	...ישי בית הלחמי (16:1b) ...ויעבר ישי שבעת בניו (16:10a)
...אליאב...אבינדב...שמה (v. 13b)	...אליאב...אבינדב...שמה (16:6a, 8a, 9a)
ודוד הוא הקטן (v. 14a)	...עוד שאר הקטן (16:11a)
לרעות את צאן אביו בית לחם (v. 15b)	...והנה רעה בצאן (16:11a)
...ויגש הפלשתי (v. 16a)	ויצא איש הבנים ממחנות פלשתים... (17:4a)
ויאמר ישי לדוד בנו קח נא לאחיך איפת הקליא הזה ועשרה לחם הזה (v. 17a)	ויקח ישי חמור לחם ונאד יין וגדי עזים אחד וישלח ביד דוד בנו אל שאול (16:20)
ושאול והמה וכל איש ישראל בעמק האלה נלחמים עם פלשתים (v. 19)	ושאול ואיש ישראל נאספו ויחנו בעמק האלה ויערכו מלחמה לקראת פלשתים (17:2)
...והרעו במלחמה (v. 20b)	...ויריעו... (17:52a)
ותערך ישראל ופלשתים מערכה לקראת מערכה (v. 21)	ויערכו מלחמה לקראת פלשתים (17:2b)
...והנה איש הבנים עולה גלית הפלשתי שמו מגת ממערות פלשתים וידבר כדברים האלה וישמע דוד (v. 23)	ויצא איש הבנים ממחנות פלשתים גלית שמו מגת (17:4a) וישמע...דברי הפלשתי האלה (17:11a)

1 Samuel 17:12–31	Source Material
וכל איש ישראל בראותם את האיש וינסו מפניו וייראו מאד (v. 24)	... וכל ישראל ... ויחתו וייראו מאד (17:11) וייראו הפלשתים כי מת גבורם וינסו (17:51b)
... כי לחרף את ישראל עלה (v. 25a)	... חרפתי את מערכות ישראל ... ... כי חרף מערכת אלהים חיים ... יהוה ... אשר חרפת (17:10a, 36b [cf. LXX], 45b)
... ואת בתו יתן לו ... (v. 25b)	ותאהב מיכל בת שאול את דוד (18:20a) ויאמר שאול אתננה לו ... (18:21a) ויתן לו שאול את מיכל בתו לאשה (18:27b)
כי מי הפלשתי הערל הזה כי חרף מערכות אלהים חיים (v. 26b)	והיה הפלשתי הערל הזה כאחד מהם כי חרף מערכת אלהים חיים (17:36b [cf. LXX])
Eliab is angry with David (v. 28)	David is chosen over Eliab (16:6–13)

The first verse of this section (1 Sam 17:12) is the clearest indication that the passage is a secondary insertion, yet because it draws from the introduction to David in chapter 16 it is in no way at odds with that material in terms of its content.[22] The summary required this sort of introductory material in order to stand on its own. Nevertheless, the placement of this summary within the larger composition of 1 Samuel 16–18 in the MT created the need to show some awareness of the presence of the introduction al-

22. Likewise, the comment about David going back and forth between his father and Saul (1 Sam 17:15) might seem like an unnecessary piece of information, as if the writer felt the need to explain how it was that David came to the battle when all along the reader would assume David's presence as Saul's armor bearer (1 Sam 16:21). While this is certainly true, there is nothing wrong about the comment. It simply offers extra information about David's ongoing role with his father's flocks.

ready provided in the previous chapter. Thus, as Tov points out, the redactor employs the demonstrative "this" (הזה) to refer the reader back to the earlier mention of David's father. The names of David's brothers (1 Sam 17:13) and the description of David as the youngest who tended the flocks (1 Sam 17:14a, 15b) all derive from chapter 16 (1 Sam 16:6, 8-9, 11).

It is true that version 1 of the story focuses more on the setting (1 Sam 17:1-11) and the duel (1 Sam 17:40-54), while the MT-only version devotes more attention to the manner in which David arrived on the scene (1 Sam 17:12-31), but this shift in version 2 does not take away from the summary hypothesis. The depiction of David's arrival is built out of the very details provided by version 1.[23] It is simply a matter of what details the writer chose to highlight in his summary. For instance, the writer takes the account of Jesse sending David to Saul (1 Sam 16:20) and reuses it to describe how Jesse sent David to his brothers (1 Sam 17:17a). Likewise, the way in which David finds the battle scene (1 Sam 17:19, 21, 23-25a) is parallel to the setting in 1 Sam 17:2, 4a, 10a, 11.[24]

The word among the men of Israel in 1 Sam 17:25 is that the king will make rich any man who defeats Goliath. He will also grant him his daughter. This is then repeated to David in particular (1 Sam 17:26-27). Since this text does not designate which daughter of Saul is in view, it is not inconsistent with Saul's offer of Merab in 1 Sam 18:17-19 or his offer of Michal in 1 Sam 17:20-27. But there is another problem. There is never any indication that Saul made David rich after his defeat of Goliath, and his offer of Merab seems more like an afterthought than a fulfillment of a promise. Furthermore, Saul's offer of Michal is only in response to Michal's love of David. This problem is alleviated when the reader realizes that the word circulating among the men of Israel in 1 Sam 17:25

---

23. Furthermore, it is difficult, if not impossible, to trace the process the other way.

24. The summary seems to presuppose the reader's awareness of 1 Sam 17:1-11 when it refers to "the battle" (1 Sam 17:13) and "the Philistine" (1 Sam 17:16), but this is only to allow the reader to view the battle scene through David's eyes. The introduction of Goliath in 1 Sam 17:23 is now a reintroduction in its present context.

was only a rumor of a reward. Their words are never found on the lips of Saul in the narrative.

Finally, Tov wonders why Eliab speaks so harshly to David in 1 Sam 17:28, but the background for the summary writer's depiction of David's older brother is located in the source material of the story in chapter 16. There the seeds of jealousy were planted when Eliab and his other brothers were passed over by Samuel in favor of their younger brother David (1 Sam 16:6–13). They stood by while David was anointed king. Thus, the author of the summary in the MT-only version infers that what began in the narrative of his source later surfaced in David's encounter with his brothers at the battle scene.

1 Samuel 17:41, 48b, 50	Source Material
וילך הפלשתי הלך וקרב אל דוד והאיש נשא הצנה לפניו (v. 41)	והיה כי קם הפלשתי וילך ויקרב לקראת דוד (17:48a) ונשא הצנה הלך לפניו (17:7b)
וימהר דוד וירץ המערכה לקראת הפלשתי (v. 48b)	...וירץ דוד ויעמד אל הפלשתי (17:51a)
ויחזק דוד מן הפלשתי בקלע ובאבן ויך את הפלשתי וימיתהו וחרב אין ביד דוד (v. 50)	...ויקח משם אבן ויקלע ויך את הפלשתי אל מצחו (17:49a) ...לא בחרב ובחנית (17:47a) ...ויקח את חרבו וישלפה מתערה וימתתהו (17:51a)

The shorter account of the duel in version 2 (summary) is based on the longer account in version 1. The most conspicuous omission in the summary of the duel is the absence of the exchange between David and Goliath in 1 Sam 17:43–47, but David's sentiments toward Goliath expressed there (1 Sam 17:46) have already surfaced earlier in the summary (1 Sam 17:26). The summary writer also takes David's words about the sword in 1 Sam 17:47 and transfers them to the narrator in 1 Sam 17:50 in order to highlight David's defeat of Goliath by divine intervention and not by the sword. The combination of version 1 and version 2 results in the impression that David killed Goliath twice (1 Sam 17:50–51), but of course, the summary was not originally intended to stand next to its source material.

1 Samuel 17:55—18:6a	Source Material
וכשוב דוד מהכות את הפלשתי... (17:57a)	וישבו בני ישראל מדלק אחרי פלשתים (17:53a)
וראש הפלשתי בידו (17:57b)	...ויכרת בה את ראשו (17:51a) ויקח דוד את ראש הפלשתי ויבאהו ירושלם (17:54a)
ויאמר דוד בן עבדך ישי בית הלחמי (17:58b)	...ויאמר הנה ראיתי בן לישי בית הלחמי... (16:18a)
ויאהב(ה)ו יהונתן כנפשו (18:1b)	...ויאהבהו מאד (16:21b) וכל ישראל ויהודה אהב את דוד (18:16a) ותאהב מיכל בת שאול את דוד (18:20a) ומיכל בת שאול אהבתהו (18:28b [cf. LXX]) ויוסף יהונתן להשביע את דוד באהבתו אתו כי אהבת נפשו אהבו (20:17) נפלאתה אהבתך לי מאהבת נשים (2 Sam 1:26b)

1 Samuel 17:55—18:6a	Source Material
18:2 (cf. 17:15)	16:11
ויכרת יהונתן ודוד ברית באהבתו אתו כנפשו (18:3)	... כי בברית יהוה הבאת את עבדך עמך (20:8a) ויכרת יהונתן עם בית דוד (20:16a) ויוסף יהונתן להשביע את דוד באהבתו אתו כי אהבת נפשו אהבו (20:17) ויכרתו שניהם ברית ... (23:18a)
ויצא דוד בכל אשר ישלחנו שאול ישכיל וישמהו שאול על אנשי המלחמה וייטב בעיני כל העם וגם בעיני עבדי שאול (18:5)	ויסרהו שאול מעמו וישמהו לו שר אלף ויצא ויבא לפני העם (18:13)
ויהי בבואם בשוב דוד מהכות את הפלשתי ... (18:6a; cf. 17:57a)	וישבו בני ישראל מדלק אחרי פלשתים (17:53a)

Once again, the inquiry about David in 1 Sam 17:55–58 is not about David as much as it is about David's father. This is not in conflict with 1 Sam 16:18. Rather, the former is based on the latter. Saul has had no reason to remember the father of his armor bearer (or that of one of his court musicians).[25] The comment about Jonathan's love for David in 1 Sam 18:1b is deeply rooted in the larger narrative of the source material. Not only does Jonathan love him (1 Sam 20:17; 2 Sam 1:26), but also all of Israel and Judah (1 Sam 18:16), including Saul's daughter Michal (1 Sam 18:20, 28), love him. Even Saul loves David initially (1 Sam 16:21). Saul's subsequent negative attitude toward David (1 Sam 17:9, 15, 29) stands in stark contrast to the way everyone else embraces him.

The covenant between David and Jonathan (1 Sam 18:3) is well known to the reader from the summary writer's source

---

25. Notice how other armor bearers in the surrounding biblical narrative are nameless (1 Sam 14:1; 17:7; see also the nameless court musician in 2 Kgs 3:15).

material in 1 Sam 20:8, 16; 23:18. Jonathan's transferal of his garment to David in 1 Sam 18:4 may be his way of saying that the throne will be David's (1 Sam 23:17). There is a similar agreement between David and Saul in 1 Sam 24:22–23. David does his best to honor his word in the subsequent narrative (2 Sam 9; 19:25–31; 21:1–15). David apparently receives a promotion in 1 Sam 18:5 (cf. 1 Sam 16:21), something that the main story notes in 1 Sam 18:13. These are not two different positions. Rather, it is simply a feature of the combination of the summary with the main story.

Textuality and the Bible

1 Samuel 18:10–11, 17–19, 21b, 29b–30	Source Material
ויהי ממחרת ותצלח רוח אלהים רעה אל שאול ויתנבא בתוך הבית ודוד מנגן בידו כיום ביום והחנית ביד שאול ויטל שאול את החנית ויאמר אכה בדוד ובקיר ויסב דוד מפניו פעמים (vv. 10–11)	ותהי רוח יהוה רעה אל שאול והוא בביתו יושב וחניתו בידו ודוד מנגן בידו (ו) ויבקש שאול להכות בחנית בדוד ובקיר ויפטר מפני שאול ויך את החנית בקיר ודוד נס וימלט בלילה הוא (19:9–10)
ויאמר שאול אל דוד הנה בתי הגדולה מרב אתה אתן לך לאשה אך היה לי לבן חיל והלחם מלחמות יהוה ושאול אמר אל תהי ידי בו ותהי בו יד פלשתים ויאמר דוד אל שאול מי אנכי ומי חיי משפחת אבי בישראל כי אהיה חתן למלך ויהי בעת תת את מרב בת שאול לדוד והיא נתנה לעדריאל המחלתי לאשה [26] (vv. 17–19)	ותאהב מיכל בת שאול את דוד ויאמר שאול אתננה לו ותהי לו למוקש ותהי בו יד פלשתים (18:20a, 21a) ... כי מלחמות יהוה אדני נלחם ... (25:28b) ויאמר דוד הנקלה בעיניכם התחתן במלך ואנכי איש רש ונקלה (18:23b) ואת חמשת בני מרב [27] בת שאול אשר ילדה לעדריאל בן ברזלי המחלתי (2 Sam 21:8b)
ויאמר שאול אל דוד בשתים תתחתן בי היום (v. 21b)	ועתה התחתן במלך (18:22b)
ויהי שאול איב את דוד כל הימים (v. 29b)	ויהי שאול עון את דוד מהיום ההוא והלאה (18:9)
ויהי מדי צאתם שכל דוד מכל עבדי שאול וייקר שמו מאד (v. 30b)	ויהי דוד לכל דרכיו משכיל ויהוה עמו וירא שאול אשר הוא משכיל מאד ויגר מפניו (18:14–15) כי הוא יוצא ובא לפניהם (18:16b)

26. Cf. 1 Sam 25:44.
27. The Leningrad Codex has מיכל here, but several witnesses read מ(י)רב.

The portion of the summary found in 1 Sam 18:10–11 is clearly based on 1 Sam 19:9–10, but its present placement within the MT comes across as somewhat premature in the flow of the narrative. Nevertheless, for someone charged with the difficult task of distributing the component parts of the summary throughout the main story, this is probably the most suitable location given Saul's negative reaction to the celebration of David's victory over Goliath (1 Sam 18:7–9). It is possible that the use of פעמים ("two times") at the end of 1 Sam 18:11 is the editor's way of showing his awareness of 1 Sam 18:10–11 and 1 Sam 19:9–10 now existing together in the MT (cf. 1 Sam 18:21b).

The language of Saul's offer of Merab in 1 Sam 18:17–19 derives from the account of his offer of Michal in 1 Sam 18:20–27. But why did the summary writer decide to change from Michal to Merab? Part of the reason may have been that to have the older daughter was considered a greater honor. Another possibility is the fact that David's relationship with Michal ultimately ends badly (2 Sam 6:16–23). The material about Merab in 1 Sam 18:19 comes from a later passage in 2 Sam 21:8 and finds a parallel in the Michal story (1 Sam 25:44). It also creates a transition between the two accounts in the present MT. The editorial addition in 1 Sam 18:21b makes the awareness of this combination explicit.

Conclusion

The story of David and Goliath now exists in two editions: (1) the earlier, shorter edition of the Hebrew text behind the LXX and (2) the later, longer edition of the MT. The second edition of the story found in the MT is not the result of a process of editorial and exegetical additions (cf. LXX and MT Jer). Rather, the MT-only material is a separate summary of the story that once had a life of its own, but it has now been inserted secondarily into the main story. This summary was not created independently of the main story as if some other oral or written source was its basis. No, the evidence suggests that the Hebrew text behind the LXX was the source for the summary.

The summary was originally meant to circulate separately, but it soon became apparent that such a small document could not survive on its own. Only inclusion within the transmission of the larger book of Samuel could guarantee its continued existence. This is comparable to the combination of other smaller works within the Hebrew Bible: the Meghilloth, the Book of the Twelve, Judges-Ruth, Jeremiah-Lamentations. As in these other works, an attempt at composition was made in the combination of the original Hebrew text and the summary. Thus, the summary was not simply inserted in toto but distributed at appropriate points throughout with minimal editing. Of course, the fact that this was a summary was soon forgotten, and the summary was read as part of the story in what became the standard rabbinic text of Samuel, giving the surface impression of doublets and inconsistencies.

5

A Study in Variant Literary Editions
The *Vorlage* of the Syriac Version of Chronicles

THE SYRIAC PESHITTA VERSION of the Hebrew Bible is for the most part a faithful rendering of a Hebrew text very close to the kind preserved in manuscript witnesses to the Masoretic Text (MT).[1] Where the Syriac varies significantly from the MT, it often has points of contact with either the Targums, most notably in the Pentateuch, or the Septuagint (LXX), most notably in Isaiah, Psalms, and Proverbs.[2] It is difficult to establish what kind of literary dependence, if any, there was between the Syriac and the Targums and what the direction of that dependence might have been.[3] On the other hand, it appears that at least some Syriac translators had access to the LXX and consulted it on occasion.[4] Of course, there are places where the Syriac is unique, either because the translator

---

1. "The Hebrew source of S was close to M" (Tov, *Textual Criticism*, 152).

2. "That the Syriac translation of certain books of the Old Testament, especially that of the Pentateuch, is not much else than a Jewish Targum has been recognized since 1859, when J. Perles wrote his *Meletemata Peschittoniana*" (Kahle, *Cairo Geniza*, 272); Würthwein, *Text of the OT*, 85–86; Baumgartner, Étude *Critique sur l'état du texte*; Delekat, "Peschitta zu Jesaja," 185–99, 321–35; Delekat, "Ein Septuagintatargum," 225–52; Lund, "Influence of the Septuagint."

3. See Dirksen, "Old Testament Peshitta," 264–85.

4. See Weitzman, "Interpretive Character of the Syriac," 594–95.

61

contributed something, or because the translator possibly followed a no longer extant Hebrew *Vorlage*.

Nowhere does a Syriac version of a biblical book differ more from the MT than in the book of Chronicles. This is due in part to the fact that the translation technique is at times similar to that of the Targum of Chronicles.[5] It is also apparent that Syriac Chronicles frequently agrees with the LXX against the MT (see *BHS* apparatus). But this agreement does not extend to 2 Chronicles 35–36 where the LXX perhaps represents a variant literary edition in Hebrew.[6] Syriac Chronicles also has a well-known tendency to harmonize with the primary source, Samuel-Kings.[7] This situation

---

5. "As early as 1870, Tötterman noticed in his dissertation on 1 Chr that the Peshitta agrees with Tg. Chronicles in its translation technique: the translator has rendered freely, deviating from the Hebrew in a number of places, omitting and adding words, and rendering in an interpretive way. This points to a Jewish translation. His conclusions were confirmed by Fränkel, who gives a detailed comparison of the Peshitta with MT. The result is a long list of cases where the Peshitta differs from MT, in paraphrastic renderings, in additions, in omissions, in assimilations to parallel passages, sometimes following MT, but in most cases Tg. Yonatan, and in avoiding anthropomorphisms. A few examples may be given: In 1 Chr 12:1 the Hebrew text beginning with *wehemma*, 'they . . .' is rendered in the Peshitta by 'and they stood before David valiantly, and if he had so desired they would have killed Saul, the son of Kish, because they were champions and warriors'. In 12:16 (Peshitta vs. 15) 'the first month' has been translated by 'the month of Nisan'. In 28:2 'for the footstool of our God' has been rendered: 'and for the place of the *šekhina* of our God'. The conclusion is that Peshitta Chronicles is 'ein reines und unverfälschtes jüdisches Targum' (Dirksen, "Old Testament Peshitta," 294–95)."

6. "G-2 Chronicles 35–36 contains several synoptic changes vis-à-vis M: 2 Chr 35:19b lacking, 35:19"a-d" (= 2 Kgs 23:24–27) added, 35:20a lacking, 36:2"a-c" (= 2 Kgs 23:31b, 32) added, 36:4 different, 36:4"a" (= 2 Kgs 23:35) added, 36:5"a-d" (= 2 Kgs 24:1–4) added. The added verses relate to Josiah's reform, while not agreeing with "G"-2 Kings (= *kaige*-Th+). In these cases, G* may reflect a different Hebrew literary edition" (Tov, *Textual Criticism*, 321). Cf. 3 Esr.

7. E.g., 1 Chr 5:26b; 6:11; 10:4–7, 9–12; 11:2–3, 11, 14, 37; 13:14; 14:11, 13; 17:8–9, 11, 19–20; 18:1, 3, 8, 10, 16; 19:1, 3, 5, 9, 15–17; 20:1, 4; 21:25; 2 Chr 1:15; 2:9, 12; 5:3–4, 9–10; 6:5–6, 9, 12, 16–17, 19, 27, 30, 32; 7:21; 8:8–9a; 9:16; 10:4–5, 16; 11:3; 13:2a; 15:16; 16:6; 18:14, 22, 30; 22:2, 6, 12; 23:14; 25:3, 19–20, 24; 26:2; 28:1, 3; 33:6, 8, 20; 34:10, 21–22. See also 1 Chr 4:24; 6:1 (Exod 6:15–16; Num 3:17); 8:1–2 (Gen 46:21); 16:13 (Ps 105:6), 27 (Ps 96:6), 33 (Ps

A Study in Variant Literary Editions

is further complicated by the fact that neither the Samuel-Kings known to the Chronicler nor the one known to the Syriac translator was necessarily identical to the Samuel-Kings now found in the MT. The book of Chronicles sometimes appears to follow a text of Samuel closer to 4QSam^a (cf. Josephus), although it is possible that 4QSam^a has been corrected on the basis of Chronicles.[8] The LXX of Samuel-Kings, which often agrees with 4QSam^a, is a mixed translation that combines sections of the Old Greek (1 Samuel; 2 Sam 1:1—11:1; 1 Kgs 2:12—21:29) with sections of a revised Greek text (2 Sam 11:2—1 Kgs 2:11; 1 Kgs 22:1—2 Kgs 25:30) for which (proto-)Lucian often supplies the Old Greek. The LXX of 1 Samuel 17-18 features a shorter edition of the David and Goliath story.[9] The LXX of 1 Kings probably represents a secondary Hebrew edition.[10]

But the above noted phenomena in Syriac Chronicles are not enough to explain the major deviations from the MT.[11] Michael Weitzman has suggested that several passages were either omitted (1 Chr 2:23, 47-49, 53, 55; 4:7-8; 7:34-38; 8:17-22; 24:27-30a; 25:5-6; 28:12-19; 2 Chr 3:9a; 4:11-17, 19-22; 29:10-19) or re-

---

96:13b). According to Klein (*1 Chronicles*, 28), this diminishes the text-critical value of Syriac Chronicles. It also reflects an early tendency to see in Chronicles a repetition rather than an interpretation of the material in Samuel-Kings (cf. the title of the book in the LXX: "Things Omitted"; see also Willi, *Chronik als Auslegung*.)

8. See Ulrich, *Dead Sea Scrolls*, 184-201; Tov, *Greek and Hebrew Bible*, 273-83.

9. Tov, *Greek and Hebrew Bible*, 333-62.

10. Tov, "Septuagint as a Source," 43-48.

11. Minuses: 1 Chr 2:23, 45, 47-49, 53, 55; 4:3b, 7-8, 13-14, 16-18, 22-23, 34-37; 5:13, 16a, b, 18a, 19b, 20a, 26a; 6:65a; 7:18b, 34-38; 8:5a, 7b-8, 17-22, 26b-27, 32b; 9:8b, 31a; 10:13b; 11:21a, 22a (cf. 2 Sam 23:20 LXX); 12:24; 21:21b; 22:7; 23:5; 24:27-30a; 25:5-6, 30-31; 28:12-19; 29:22b, 29b; 2 Chr 2:6b; 3:2, 9a; 4:3, 5b, 11-17, 19-22; 5:12-13; 6:13a; 7:6a; 8:9b, 18a; 9:10a, 25, 29; 11:1—12:12; 13:2b, 13-14; 16:8a; 20:22-23; 24:11a, 13-14; 25:22; 26:7-8a, 11b, 15a, 17b-18a; 27:8; 28:12b, 13b, 14; 29:10-19; 30:8b; 31:2b; 32:28b; 36:8a. Pluses: 1 Chr 4:30 (cf. Josh 15:27, 31); 6:11; 12:6; 17:3b; 18:8b, 13a; 22:2 (cf. 2 Chr 2:16-17), 10a; 23:4; 26:1b; 29:18; 2 Chr 3:3b (cf. 1 Kgs 6:2); 7:10b; 20:21b (also nonn Mss). (Re)arrangement: 1 Chr 3:7-8; 4:24-25; 6:63-64; 11:43-44; 2 Chr 28:16-21.

constructed (1 Chr 12:23; 29:7) because the *Vorlage* was illegible.¹² While this is plausible in some instances, other examples appear to be due to unintentional errors like homoioteleuton (e.g., 1 Chr 2:23) or homoioarchton (e.g., 2 Chr 4:11–17). Furthermore, why would Syriac Chronicles out of all of the books of the Syriac Peshitta suddenly suffer from an illegible *Vorlage* to this extent? Could not the illegible sections have been supplied from the LXX version that the translator used as a resource? Surely the exact same sections were not illegible there as well.

One option that has not been explored is the possibility that Syriac Chronicles bears witness to a variant literary edition of Chronicles in Hebrew. A variant literary edition goes beyond the level of individual readings to that of a reworked version of a section or whole book involving such things as large-scale omissions, additions, and rearrangements.¹³ Variant literary editions are attested for most of the books of the Hebrew Bible, most notably Jeremiah, so the lack of such an edition for the book of Chronicles would actually be the exception rather than the rule. If witnesses like 4QJudgᵃ and 4QCantᵃ are enough to suggest variant literary editions, then surely the unique minuses, pluses, and reworkings that run throughout Syriac Chronicles warrant examination to determine whether or not it represents such an edition.

First Chronicles 2:47–49

This passage appears to be a secondary insertion in the MT and does not occur in the Syriac. It begins with a list of the sons of Jahdai (1 Chr 2:47) who is not one of the descendants of Caleb listed in 1 Chr 2:42–46. The passage was apparently thought to be relevant to the list of Caleb's sons because of the mention of the sons of Caleb's concubine Maacah in 1 Chr 2:48–49 and also because of the mention of Caleb's daughter Achsah at the end of 1 Chr 2:49. But the beginning of 1 Chr 2:50 ("These were the sons of

---

12. Weitzman, "Interpretive Character of the Syriac," 596.

13. See Tov, *Textual Criticism*, 283–326; Ulrich, *Dead Sea Scrolls*, 17–33, 106–9.

A Study in Variant Literary Editions

Caleb") clearly presupposes that the list in 1 Chr 2:42-46, which has Caleb's sons, and not the one in 1 Chr 2:47-49, which begins with Jahdai's sons, has preceded it. The beginning of 1 Chr 2:50 is not an introduction to what follows (i.e., the list of the sons of Hur) but a conclusion to what comes before it. The *waw* at the beginning of 1 Chr 2:47 suggests that 1 Chr 2:47-49 has been lifted from another source where it was part of a larger context. Thus, in this case the shorter text of the Syriac Peshitta represents the more original version.[14]

First Chronicles 4:3b, 7-8, 13-14, 16-18, 22-23, 34-37

These verses missing from the Syriac version show that a substantial revision of the genealogies of Judah and Simeon took place before they reached the form that they have in the MT.[15] There is nothing from the content of these verses that would suggest a deliberate attempt to omit them. It is possible that the material in 1 Chr 4:13-14, 16-18 was omitted by accident (homoioarchton; cf. 1 Chr 7:34-38), but the fact is that the tendency to fill out the genealogies in the MT of 1 Chronicles 1-9 is quite noticeable (e.g., 1 Chr 2:53, 55; 5:13, 16a, b, 18a, 19b, 20a, 26a; 6:65a; 7:18b, 34-38; 8:5a, 7b-8, 17-22, 26b-27, 32b; 9:8b, 31a). By contrast the pluses in this section of the Syriac version are slight (e.g., 1 Chr 4:30 [cf. Josh 15:27, 31]; 6:11).[16]

---

14. It is also worth noting that the Chronicler does not customarily dwell on the concubines of his heroes, although he does mention Ephah in this context (1 Chr 2:46). For example, 1 Kgs 11:3 and the surrounding context of the Chronicler's source material are not in his account of Solomon.

15. 1 Chronicles 4:22 makes reference to "ancient words," possibly indicating another source. The names referenced in 1 Chr 4:38 were presumably the ones in 1 Chr 4:24-33 before the addition of a separate and unmarked list in 1 Chr 4:34-37.

16. It is not clear whether the arrangements in 1 Chr 3:7-8; 4:24-25; 6:63-64 should be dubbed rearrangements.

First Chronicles 10–21

This is the section of narrative material in 1 Chronicles where the Chronicler is most dependent on Samuel. The following account of David's preparations for Solomon's temple (1 Chr 22–29) does not come from Samuel-Kings. It is striking then that 1 Chronicles 10–21 has a relatively low number of minuses (and pluses) in the Syriac version. Whereas the MT expands freely on the genealogies in 1 Chronicles 1–9, it generally respects the relationship between the Chronicler and Samuel, leaving the treatment of the source material there more or less untouched. The additions that do occur in the MT in comparison with the Syriac seem to be of the usual sort of textual variation rather than anything that would be indicative of a variant literary edition. For example, the absence of *lidrosh* ("to seek") at the end of 1 Chr 10:13 in the Syriac is probably original. It was likely added at some point by someone who read *lishol* ("to ask") earlier in the verse as *leshaul* ("to Saul") and thus needed to supply an infinitive (see 1 Sam 28:7).[17] The heading in the MT of 1 Chr 12:24 is another instance. It does not occur in the Syriac and appears to be an isolated editorial addition.[18]

---

17. Klein (*1 Chronicles*, 283) considers the present MT to be a conflation of synonymous readings for which it is impossible to determine the original. Of course, Talmon (*Text and Canon*, 171–266) has long argued that such readings originated together and reflect good Hebrew style. The decision to choose one over the other is according to this view a secondary move by early translators like those of the LXX. But the inability to choose between two readings is not necessarily an indication that there was no linear development (Tov, *Textual Criticism*, 164).

18. See also 1 Chr 18:8b, 13a. Both the Syriac and the LXX have shorter texts for 1 Chr 21:21b, but they are shorter in different places in the verse. The LXX does not have, "and Arnon looked and saw David" (cf. 2 Sam 24:20: "and Araunah looked out his window and saw the king and his servants crossing over to him"). The Syriac does not have, "and he went forth from the threshing floor" (cf. 2 Sam 24:20: "and Araunah went forth"; see also 4QSam^a).

A Study in Variant Literary Editions

First Chronicles 22:7

The absence of 1 Chr 22:7 ("And David said to Solomon, 'My son, as for me, it was with my heart to build a house for the name of YHWH my God'") from the Syriac version is a curious example in part because its inclusion in the MT is apparently not part of a systematic revision of the chapter as a whole. There seems to be no reason why the Syriac translator would have intentionally omitted the verse had it been present in his *Vorlage*. The same thought is expressed by David in 1 Chr 28:2 using similar terminology and is not lacking in the Syriac. Of course, the MT does not read smoothly from 1 Chr 22:6 directly into 1 Chr 22:8 without verse 7, but the Syriac version does not have this problem. Verse 6 in the Syriac already begins David's discourse with Solomon in which he instructs his son to build the temple. Verse 8 then continues the thought with the following: "because he sent to me by the hand of a prophet and said to me . . . " Indications of an accidental omission are scant, although it is possible that the translator could have skipped from the end of 1 Chr 22:6 to the end of 1 Chr 22:7 if his *Vorlage* read "my God" instead of "the God of Israel" at the end of 1 Chr 22:6 or "the God of Israel" instead of "my God" at the end of 1 Chr 22:7. This could have stemmed from an original abbreviation of "Israel" using the letter *yodh*.[19] But this is purely hypothetical. The other, perhaps more likely, option is that the edition of the book represented by the MT has added 1 Chr 22:7 on the basis of the parallel in 1 Chr 28:2. This then allowed for (and required) a revision of verses 6 and 8. This sort of practice is known to occur in expansions of other books (e.g., Ezek 2:3-5; 3:7, LXX and MT).[20]

---

19. See Tov, *Textual Criticism*, 238-39; Talmon, *Text and Canon*, 269-71.

20. The LXX of Ezekiel is about four to five percent shorter than the MT in large part because of this kind of extraction from similar contexts in the MT (see Lilly, *Two Books of Ezekiel*).

First Chronicles 23:4–5; 24:27–30a; 25:1, 5–6, 30–31; 28:12–19

It is not always possible to see how or why the differences between the Syriac and the MT may have originated. For instance, the Syriac has the longer text for 1 Chr 23:4, but it lacks 1 Chr 23:5. Is the former an expansion (cf. 1 Chr 26:1; 29:18) and the latter an original reading? Likewise, the absence of 1 Chr 24:27–30a in the Syriac could be the result of homoioarchton, but its presence in the MT could be the result of a deliberate attempt to complete the genealogy of Merari (cf. 1 Chr 1–9). The Syriac version of 1 Chr 25:1 differs considerably from the MT and does not include the description of the musicians as those who would prophesy on their instruments (cf. 2 Kgs 3:15). In that same chapter (1 Chr 25), verses 5 and 6 appear to be added commentary on the sons of Heman in the MT. The Syriac has the shorter reading. But the absence of 1 Chr 25:30–31 in the Syriac is likely an accidental omission due to homoioteleuton since 1 Chr 25:1–6 provides a list of twenty-four rather than twenty-two sons of Asaph, Heman, and Jeduthun. The Syriac version of 1 Chr 25:4 does have a shorter list for the sons of Heman (six names instead of fourteen), but this makes for a total of sixteen names in 1 Chr 25:2–4—an internal contradiction to the number twenty-two with which the Syriac ends in 1 Chr 25:29.

The Syriac and the MT both have expansions on 1 Chr 28:11. The shorter expansion in the Syriac is in the second half of its version of 1 Chr 28:11. The longer expansion in the MT is in 1 Chr 28:12–19 (based on Exod 25:9, 40), verses that do not appear in the Syriac. The original version of 1 Chronicles 28 probably read straight from verse 11 to verse 20. Other additions (e.g., 1 Chr 29:22, 29) in the MT of 1 Chronicles 22–29 as compared to the Syriac are traceable to known passages elsewhere (e.g., 2 Sam 7; 12; 1 Chr 23:1). Thus, the Syriac does not always represent the more original edition in this section, and the MT is somewhat more restrained than it was in 1 Chronicles 1–9, but the MT still does not hesitate to expand and/or comment when necessary.

A Study in Variant Literary Editions

Second Chronicles 4:3, 5b, 11-17, 19-22; 5:12-13; 9:25, 29

The MT of 2 Chronicles 1-9 shows more willingness to add to source material from the section devoted to Solomon in 1 Kings 1-11, more so than it did with the material from Samuel in 1 Chronicles 10-21. With all due respect to minor additions like 2 Chr 3:9a; 7:6a, which do not appear in the Syriac, the most dramatic difference between the MT and the Syriac in 2 Chronicles 1-9 is in chapter 4. The Syriac version of this chapter lacks verses 3, 5b, 11-17, and 19-22. It is possible that verses 11-17 were accidentally omitted when the scribe or translator skipped from the first word of verse 11 to the first word of verse 18. After all, verse 18 seems to refer to the bronze vessels in verse 16. On the other hand, the word "vessel" can refer to a wide range of objects (BDB, 479-80), and verses 1-9 of chapter 4 begin with reference to a bronze altar and end with reference to doors overlaid with bronze. Moreover, homoioarchton would not explain the omission of verses 19-22. It seems at least equally plausible that the MT has filled out the description of Hiram's work from 1 Kings 7. Thus, this would be a case where the MT does not add to the source material. Rather, it adds to the earlier edition of Chronicles from the source material in Kings.

But 2 Chr 5:12-13 is clearly an addition in the MT to the source material in 1 Kings 8, one that does not occur in the Syriac. The text of 2 Chr 5:11a, 14 is virtually identical to that of 1 Kgs 8:10a, 11, but the difference between 2 Chr 5:11b and 1 Kgs 8:10b has prompted the addition in 2 Chr 5:12-13. In the original text(s), the focus of the narrative is the cloud filling the temple upon the departure of the priests, which made it impossible for the priests to remain. This part of the narrative reads continuously in 1 Kgs 8:10-11 (cf. 2 Chr 5:11a, 14). The Chronicler, however, has introduced a comment about the priests in 2 Chr 5:11b, which does not appear in 1 Kgs 8:10b. This comment paved the way for the MT to incorporate an expansion on the priests in 2 Chr 5:12-13, interrupting the focus on the cloud filling the temple. The material for this expansion was apparently borrowed from 1 Chronicles 25.

The MT of 2 Chr 9:25, 29 features both practices observed above—supplementation from source material and addition to source material. These two verses do not appear in the Syriac version. The MT has supplied 2 Chr 9:25a from 1 Kgs 5:6 with an expansion in 2 Chr 9:25b. The source citation in the MT of 2 Chr 9:29, however, completely differs from 1 Kgs 11:41.

> And the rest of the things of Solomon and all that he did and his wisdom, are they not written in the book of the things of Solomon (1 Kgs 11:41)?
> And the rest of the things of Solomon, the former and the latter, are they not written in the things of Nathan the prophet and in the prophecy of Ahijah the Shilonite and in the visions of Iddo the seer concerning Jeroboam the son of Nebat (2 Chr 9:29)?

The "things of Nathan the prophet" are referenced in 1 Chr 29:29 (MT) but not in the book of Kings, although they would presumably include material such as what is found in texts like 2 Samuel 7; 12; 1 Kings 1. The "prophecy of Ahijah" is in 1 Kgs 11:29-39, but it does not occur in Chronicles (cf. 2 Chr 10:15). The "visions of Iddo" are not referenced in the book of Kings (but see 1 Kgs 13:1-10; *Ant.* 8:231-35), but Iddo's name appears in two other source citations in Chronicles (2 Chr 12:15; 13:22). It might seem odd that the Syriac version does not include any source citation in its conclusion to the account of Solomon, but if it does represent an earlier edition of the book of Chronicles, it is possible that the Chronicler assumed his audience knew his source from 1 Chr 29:29 (cf. 1 Sam 10:25)—a source citation not found in Samuel-Kings, thus necessitating the one in 1 Kgs 11:41.

Second Chronicles 11:1—12:12; 13:2b, 13-14; 20:22-23

The longest continuous section not included in Syriac Chronicles is 2 Chr 11:1—12:12. The first part of this section in 2 Chr 11:1-4 is material from 1 Kgs 12:21-24. The remainder of 2 Chronicles 11 is not from any extant source, but 2 Chr 12:15 cites the words of Shemaiah and Iddo for the stories about Rehoboam. The section in 2 Chr 11:5-23 does seem to show some awareness of the description of Jeroboam in 1 Kgs 12:25-33. Its interest in Judah and Jerusalem and their superiority to the northern kingdom of Israel would seem to go well with the Chronicler's purposes, and there is little reason why someone would deliberately omit the passage if it were original. Furthermore, there are no signs of accidental omission on the part of a scribe or the Syriac translator.

After the introduction in 2 Chr 12:1 (cf. 1 Kgs 14:22-24), the text of 2 Chr 12:2-12 offers an expanded version of the story in 1 Kgs 14:25-28:

> Between the first and last three verses of that account (1 Kgs 14:25, 26-28 // 2 Chr 12:2a, 9aβb-11) the Chronicler has inserted materials that identify the people's unfaithfulness, provide more details of the invasion, and describe a prophetic judgment speech and its consequences (vv. 2b-8). Verse 3 provides new information about the numbers and the ethnic identity of Shishak's troops, while v. 4 reports that Shishak captured the cities of defense that Rehoboam had built (cf. 2 Chr 11:5-12). A prophetic speech (vv. 5-8) is delivered by Shemaiah, who has already been introduced in 2 Chr 11:2-4 // 1 Kgs 12:22-24. Verse 9aα repeats v. 2a (*Wiederaufnahme*; repetitive resumption) and allows the Chronicler to include additional verses (vv. 9aβ-11) dealing with this invasion taken from 1 Kgs 14:26-28. Verse 12, added by the Chronicler, reports additional effects of the people's repentance.[21]

It is possible that this negative account of a Judean king was simply not welcome in the *Vorlage* of the Syriac, but the failures of Rehoboam are already well known to the reader from 2 Chronicles 10. It is more likely that 2 Chr 12:1-12 was a later addition to the book. The passage is somewhat out of character with the Chronicler's use of material from Samuel and Kings elsewhere (cf. 1 Chr 10-21). The Chronicler is ordinarily more subtle. For example, the

---

21. Klein, *2 Chronicles*, 180.

text of 2 Chr 12:13-15 takes considerably less liberties with the source material in 2 Kgs 14:21-22, 29-31.

The text of 2 Kgs 15:6 (> Old Greek) and 2 Chr 13:2b (> Syriac) is generally considered a misplaced doublet of 1 Kgs 14:30 and 2 Chr 12:15 (cf. 1 Kgs 15:7; 2 Chr 13:22). The account of Abijah in 2 Chr 13:4-21 does not come from the book of Kings, but it is not unusual for the Chronicler to supplement the accounts of Judean kings (e.g., Asa [2 Chr 14-16; cf. 1 Kgs 15:9-24], Jehoshaphat [2 Chr 17-20; cf. 1 Kgs 22:41-51], and Hezekiah [2 Chr 29-32; cf. 2 Kgs 18-20]), given the fact that he does not devote the space to the kings of the north like the book of Kings does. The first two verses of the battle report in 2 Chr 13:13-21 are missing in the Syriac version. It is not difficult to read straight from the end of the discourse in 2 Chr 13:12 into the narration in 2 Chr 13:15. Verses 13 and 14 supply background information ("x + qtl" [v. 13a]) for the narration. This is consistent with the overall character of the second edition of Chronicles as represented by the MT, which tends to provide context for the reader. The same can be said of verses 22 and 23 in chapter 20, which are absent from the Syriac. They provide background information ("x + qtl" [v. 22a]) for the account of the war.

Second Chronicles 24:11a, 13-14; 25:22; 26:7-8a, 11b, 15a, 17b-18a; 27:8

The story of Joash in 2 Chronicles 24 is clearly a reading of the story in 2 Kings 12, but the Chronicler's account differs in detail at several points. Verse 11 is a reworking of 2 Kgs 12:11. The Syriac has the shorter version of this reworking, which the MT has expanded. Verse 13 of 2 Chronicles 24 does not have a parallel in 2 Kings 12. It also does not occur in the Syriac of Chronicles. It is likely an addition to the work of the Chronicler based on texts like Exod 25:9, 40; Ezek 43:10 (cf. 1 Chr 28:11). Verse 14 of 2 Chronicles 24

A Study in Variant Literary Editions

appears on the surface to be in contradiction to what 2 Kgs 12:14 says. Thus, the absence of this verse in the Syriac version would seem to be a deliberate attempt to avoid such an embarrassment. On the other hand, the verse could be a secondary and unwittingly erroneous addition designed to boast the amount of money brought for temple repairs (cf. Exod 35:4—36:7; 1 Chr 29:6-9).

The second half of the story of Amaziah in 2 Chr 25:14-28 highlights the failures of the Judean king. The statement about the defeat of Judah at the hands of Jehoash the king of Israel in 2 Chr 25:22 is in the source text (2 Kgs 14:12), but it is not in the Syriac version of Chronicles. While the Chronicler does mention the failures of Judean kings elsewhere (e.g, Joash, Uzziah, Manasseh), he generally presents the Davidic monarchy in a more positive light than the book of Kings does. This is because his trajectory primarily extends to what lies beyond the Babylonian exile (2 Chr 36:22-23) rather than what leads up to it (2 Kgs 25:27-30). The statement in 2 Chr 25:22 makes explicit what would only be implicit without it. Its absence takes some of the sting out of the account of Judah's defeat. It is plausible that the Chronicler never intended to include the verse and that it is in the MT only because it was added secondarily on the basis of 2 Kgs 14:12. But this does not rule out the possibility that the Syriac translator or the scribe responsible for his *Vorlage* took exception to the verse and deleted it.

The Syriac version of the Uzziah story in 2 Chronicles 26 is significantly shorter than the one in the MT. The account of Uzziah's faithfulness in 2 Chr 26:5-15 does not appear in the parallel story about Uzziah in 2 Kings 15. The absence of 2 Chr 26:7 in the Syriac is striking because the attribution of Uzziah's defeat of the Philistines to divine aid is consistent with the theology of the Chronicler's sources and his own work in general (e.g., 1 Kgs 12:15, 22-24; 1 Chr 10:15; 2 Chr 20:15). There seems to be little reason why the Syriac translator or the scribe responsible for his *Vorlage* would have omitted it on purpose. It is likely an addition based on the use of the Hebrew word "help" (*azar*) elsewhere in the chapter—a play on Uzziah's name Azariah in 2 Kings 15 (2 Chr 26:7, 13, 15, 17).[22]

It is difficult to say why the material in 2 Chr 26:11b, 15a is not in the Syriac version other than the likely fact that it simply was not present in the translator's *Vorlage*. The second edition of the book of Chronicles has thus far shown itself to be one in which a fuller account is given wherever possible. The same is true for 2 Chr 26:17b–18a, although there the added text is part of a section (2 Chr 26:16–21) in which the Chronicler himself is giving a fuller account of what is referenced very briefly in 2 Kgs 15:5.[23]

Second Chronicles 28:12b, 13b, 14, 16–21

The Syriac version of the story of Ahaz in 2 Chronicles 28 is not only shorter than the version in the MT—lacking verses 12b, 13b, and 14—but also it is in a different arrangement, placing verses 16–21 between verses 25 and 26. The section in 2 Chr 28:12–21 does not have an exact parallel in the accounts of Ahaz in 2 Kings 16 or Isaiah 7, although there are some similarities in detail. Verses 16–21 provide the key to understanding the history of this chapter's development. According to these verses, Ahaz made his

---

22. The addition in 2 Chr 26:8a ("And the Ammonites gave tribute to Uzziah") appears to be related to the end of the addition in 2 Chr 26:7, which refers to the Meunim. The Chronicler normally uses "the sons of Ammon" rather "Ammonites," so the secondary nature of the text is evident. The LXX attempts to correct this problem by changing "Ammonites" to "Meunim," relieving the text of an otherwise random reference to the Ammonites (cf. 2 Chr 20:1). Another possibility is that "Ammonites" arose by graphic confusion of "Meunim." A few manuscripts have "Ammonites" at the end of verse 7, perhaps because the name is more familiar than "Meunim." See also 1 Chr 4:41.

23. 2 Chronicles 27:8, which is included in the sub-heading for this section, is not discussed here because the Syriac is not alone in its omission of the verse. The entire verse is lacking in the LXX and is generally considered secondary (see Klein, *2 Chronicles*, 388). It is difficult to say whether or not the Syriac and LXX bear independent witness to an earlier, shorter Hebrew text. Given the Syriac's dependence on the LXX elsewhere, it is possible that the translator simply followed his Greek model. But the consistently shorter text of Syriac Chronicles gives strong indication that the translator might have worked from his own shorter *Vorlage* here.

A Study in Variant Literary Editions

appeal to Tiglath-pileser due to threats from the Edomites and the Philistines, but the accounts in 2 Kings 16 and Isaiah 7 suggest that the real threat was in the alliance between Ephraim and Syria. While it is possible that Ahaz faced threats from all sides, the secondary nature of the passage in Chronicles is evident from the two different placements of the unit in the MT and the Syriac.[24] The passage was probably added as an appendix to an earlier edition of 2 Chronicles 28 represented by the Syriac version, which is why it appears in that version after verse 25 and directly before the source citation and death notice for Ahaz in 2 Chr 28:26-27. The reason for this addition may have been to parallel the reference to Tiglath-pileser in 2 Kings 16, overlooking the differences in detail. In a later edition of the book of Chronicles represented by the MT, that passage was relocated to fit within the flow of the narrative between verses 15 and 22.

Second Chronicles 29:10-19; 30:8b

The account of Hezekiah's temple repairs, Passover celebration, and religious reforms in 2 Chronicles 29-31 finds no parallel in 2 Kings 18-20 or Isaiah 36-39. Hezekiah's story in 2 Kings and Isaiah appears in an abbreviated form in 2 Chronicles 32. The section in 2 Chr 29:10-19, which is missing from the Syriac version, features Hezekiah's covenant with YHWH in response to the sins of the forefathers. This covenant is made in the hearing of the Levites who then rise up to aid Hezekiah. The story is remarkably similar to the one in Exod 32:26-29 where the Levites come to the aid of Moses in response to the golden calf incident. Hezekiah is elsewhere in 2 Chr 30:14 depicted as a Moses-like figure in language borrowed from the golden calf story (Exod 32:20; Deut 9:21; 1 Kgs 15:13; 2 Kgs 23:4, 6, 12, 15; 2 Chr 15:16; 34:4).[25] This passage in 2 Chr 29:10-19 is also similar to other late additions to the biblical text designed to promote the interests of the Levites (e.g., Jer

---

24. Klein does not believe the attacks by the Edomites and the Philistines are historical (*2 Chronicles*, 394-95).

25. See Shepherd, *Text in the Middle*, 78-80.

33:14–26 > LXX). Such an addition was likely prompted by the work of the Chronicler himself whose own interest in the temple, the priests, and the Levites of his day is reflected in his depiction of the past (e.g., 2 Chr 29:34).²⁶

The expression "give hand to YHWH" (LXX: "give glory to the Lord God"; cf. Josh 7:19) in 2 Chr 30:8b is absent from the Syriac. To give hand apparently means to make a pledge (cf. Ezra 10:19), but the expression may have been unfamiliar to the Syriac translator, as it was to the LXX translator, or to the scribe responsible for his *Vorlage*. There is no indication that it was accidentally omitted, nor is there any reason to think that it was deliberately omitted on grounds that it would be objectionable in some way. The expression was simply not understandable and therefore not transmitted under the assumption that it was unnecessary to the intelligibility of the passage. Or, the Syriac translator was not as bold as the LXX translator to venture a guess, even with a word-for-word translation. Perhaps the feeling was that deletion of the expression would be better than misrepresentation.

Conclusion

Because the Syriac Peshitta version of the Hebrew Bible is generally a faithful rendering of a text close to the MT, any major deviations from what occurs in the MT would presumably be due to the presence of a different Hebrew *Vorlage* rather than the work of the translator himself.²⁷ Given the widespread recognition of targumic renderings and the influence of the LXX on the Syriac Peshitta, it is important to rule out both in any instance of textual variation from the MT before entertaining the option of a different

---

26. Other scholars have suspected the reference to the Levites in this section to be secondary. See Büchler, "Zur Geschichte der Tempelmusik," 109–14; Welch, *Work of the Chronicler*, 103–8; Peterson, *Late Israelite Prophecy*, 77–85.

27. ". . . when we find major deviations from the MT in a faithful translation, they probably reflect a different Hebrew text. On the other hand, if a translator was not faithful to his parent text in small details, even paraphrasing it occasionally, he could have inserted major changes in the translation" (Tov, "Septuagint as a Source," 33).

A Study in Variant Literary Editions

Vorlage. The Syriac version of Chronicles presents the critic with this option more than any other book in the Peshitta.

Several large-scale observations can be made about Syriac Chronicles. First, the MT tends to expand somewhat freely on the genealogies in 1 Chronicles 1–9 in contrast to the Syriac version. On the other hand, the Syriac and the MT both have a relatively low number of minuses and pluses in 1 Chronicles 10–21, respecting the relationship between the Chronicler and the biblical source material in Samuel. The Syriac does not always represent the more original edition in 1 Chronicles 22–29, and the MT is somewhat more restrained than it was in 1 Chronicles 1–9, but the MT does not hesitate to expand when it is considered necessary.

The MT of 2 Chronicles 1–9 shows more willingness to add to source material from the section devoted to Solomon in 1 Kings 1–11, more so than it did with the material from Samuel in 1 Chronicles 10–21. In fact, the MT consistently has the longer text in 2 Chronicles in comparison to the Syriac version, and there is usually some indication from the context that the longer text is due to deliberate addition in the MT rather than unintentional or intentional omission on the part of the Syriac or its source. Given the global nature of the type and extent of differences between MT Chronicles and Syriac Chronicles, it is difficult to avoid the conclusion that Syriac Chronicles represents an earlier Hebrew edition of the book. The second edition of the book of Chronicles represented by the MT is one in which a fuller account is given wherever possible.[28]

---

28. On the subject of multiple editions, see Martin, *Multiple Originals*.

6

A Grammatical Study
The Object Marker for the Preposition את in Later Biblical Hebrew

THE OBJECT MARKER את often appears in MT in place of the preposition את, frequently with textual variation:[1]

ויקח אֹתָהּ וישכב אֹתָהּ ויענה
And he took her and lay her (LXX: with her [μετ' αὐτῆς = אִתָּהּ]) and humbled her (Gen 34:2b)[2]

והתחתנו אֹתָנוּ
And intermarry us (Syr., Tgg.: with us = אִתָּנוּ)
(Gen 34:9a)

According to Takamitsu Muraoka, only Samaritan Hebrew and Babylonian Hebrew keep the object marker and the preposition apart.[3] The object marker for the preposition occurs primarily (not only) in late pre-exilic to early post-exilic Hebrew (Kgs, Jer, and Ezek). Shelomo Morag's study of the phenomenon concludes that the occurrences in Ezekiel and Second Isaiah are Akkadianisms,

---

1. See BDB, 85–87; *HALOT*, 101.

2. Neither *qal* שכב nor English "lay" (cf. laid) is transitive, thus the problem. In this case a "correct" use of the object marker is followed by a supposedly "incorrect" one. The LXX reflects a different vocalization of the same consonants (cf. Syr., *Tg. Neof.* [עמה], and Vulg.).

3. Joüon and Muraoka, *Grammar of Biblical Hebrew*, 315, n. 6.

A Grammatical Study

while those in the books of Kings and Jeremiah are Aramaisms.[4] Muraoka, however, notes that the *nota accusativi* is not frequent in contemporary Aramaic documents. He prefers an explanation from מאת in which את is weakened.

In his *Historical Grammar of Biblical Hebrew*, Alexander Sperber lists places where *BHK* "corrects" the use of the object marker in place of the preposition.[5] He classifies these according to main verb and other syntactical relationships:

w/שכב: Gen 34:2; Num 5:13, 19; 2 Sam 13:14; Ezek 23:8

w/דבר: 1 Kgs 22:24; Ezek 2:1; 3:22, 24, 27; 14:4; 44:5; 2 Chr 18:23

w/עשה: Jer 21:2; Ezek 16:59; 20:17; 22:14; 23:25, 29; 39:24

w/דרש: 1 Kgs 22:7-8; 2 Kgs 3:11; 8:8

w/ל הם: Josh 10:25; 1 Kgs 20:25

w/ברית: Isa 59:21; Ezek 16:8, 60; 37:26

other: (1) Josh 14:12; Jer 10:5; 20:11; (2) 2 Kgs 1:15; Ezek 10:17; (3) Gen 34:9; 2 Sam 24:24; (4) 2 Kgs 3:12, 26; 6:16; Ezek 23:23; 38:9; Job 32:6

This classification is a helpful starting point for examination of what appears on the surface to be confusion between the object marker and the preposition את.

The present chapter seeks to explain the use of the object marker for the preposition את from the increasing disuse of the preposition in transitional and late biblical Hebrew, perhaps under the influence of Aramaic, which prefers עם.[6] Such a linguistic environment would have led to the misunderstanding of the preposition and the misuse of the object marker. The following discussion surveys the vast majority of occurrences and analyzes their

---

4. Morag, "Tiberian Tradition of Biblical Hebrew," 105–44.
5. Sperber, *Historical Grammar of Biblical Hebrew*, 63–64.
6. Muraoka counts thirteen occurrences of the preposition in Esther, Ezra, Daniel, and Chronicles out of over nine hundred occurrences in the Hebrew Bible (Joüon and Muraoka, *Grammar of Biblical Hebrew*, 316). Parallel to this is the decreased use of the object marker with pronominal suffixes (see Rooker, *Biblical Hebrew in Transition*, 45).

syntactical settings and textual histories. Consistent usage in later books, orthography, and clues from the textual witnesses provide the necessary information to explain what otherwise seems to be rather haphazard.

Distribution of את

The following shows the distribution of the object marker את in *BHS* according to *Accordance* (Groves-Wheeler Westminster Hebrew Morphology):

Book	Count	Book	Count
Genesis	1012	Micah	16
Exodus	1026	Nahum	1
Leviticus	772	Habakkuk	4
Numbers	702	Zephaniah	22
Deuteronomy	653	Haggai	18
Joshua	563	Zechariah	97
Judges	466	Malachi	35
1 Samuel	540	Psalms	150
2 Samuel	400	Job	46
1 Kings	554	Proverbs	21
2 Kings	588	Ruth	32
Isaiah	223	Song	24
Jeremiah	858	Ecclesiastes	74
Ezekiel	645	Lamentations	7
Hosea	45	Esther	115
Joel	18	Daniel	38
Amos	45	Ezra	30
Obadiah	9	Nehemiah	129
Jonah	14	1 Chronicles	457
		2 Chronicles	531

A Grammatical Study

Taking into account the fact that poetic texts tend to use the object marker less than prose texts,[7] the marker is nevertheless well represented throughout the Tanakh. Genesis–Ezekiel and Chronicles have the vast majority of occurrences.

The distribution of the preposition אֵת is quite a bit different from that of the object marker:

Book	Count	Book	Count
Genesis	135	Micah	4
Exodus	44	Nahum	0
Leviticus	26	Habakkuk	1
Numbers	52	Zephaniah	1
Deuteronomy	27	Haggai	3
Joshua	28	Zechariah	15
Judges	36	Malachi	3
1 Samuel	43	Psalms	25
2 Samuel	61	Job	6
1 Kings	45	Proverbs	25
2 Kings	58	Ruth	8
Isaiah	47	Song	2
Jeremiah	96	Ecclesiastes	0
Ezekiel	54	Lamentations	0
Hosea	2	Esther	4
Joel	0	Daniel	2
Amos	1	Ezra	2
Obadiah	1	Nehemiah	6
Jonah	0	1 Chronicles	6
		2 Chronicles	19

---

7. See Freedman, "Pottery, Poetry, and Prophecy," 5–26.

According to the general consensus, pre-exilic biblical Hebrew occurs in Genesis–Numbers (minus P), Deuteronomy–2 Kings 23, Isaiah 1–39, Hosea, Amos, Obadiah, and Micah–Zephaniah.[8] Late pre-exilic to early post-exilic biblical Hebrew occurs in 2 Kings 24–25, Isaiah 40–55, Jeremiah, Ezekiel, and Lamentations. Post-exilic biblical Hebrew occurs in the P material of the Pentateuch, Isaiah 56–66, Haggai–Malachi, Ecclesiastes, and Esther–Chronicles.[9] Of course, it is necessary to take into account the influence of earlier idiom on later writing as well as the updating of earlier texts. It is also possible to debate about the location of some texts such as the P material. But overall this model seems to do justice to the evidence.

The preposition את occurs in pre-exilic biblical Hebrew much more than transitional or post-exilic biblical Hebrew, although it is well represented in Jeremiah and Ezekiel. The real decline in usage occurs in post-exilic biblical Hebrew. Only Chronicles has somewhat of a substantial number (25/948), but it is still meager. Even this number is likely due to the influence of the Chronicler's sources such as Samuel and Kings whose total number of occurrences (207/948) makes that of Chronicles pale in comparison. In contrast to usage of the object marker, the preposition את does not appear in Mishnaic Hebrew.[10] It also does not appear in Aramaic (but see Akkadian *itti*, Phoenician *'t*, and Ethiopic *'enta* ["towards"]). The preposition does appear, however, in the Hebrew of the Dead Sea Scrolls (e.g., 1QS 6:2–3, 12–13; 7:5, 16; 8:20; 9:19; 10:18; 1QM 4:2; 7:5–6; 11:4; 12:2, 8; 18:6; 19:1; 1QH[a]

---

8. See Miller-Naudé and Zevit, *Diachrony in Biblical Hebrew*; Naudé, "Linguistic Dating of Biblical Hebrew," 1–22; Young et al., *Linguistic Dating of Biblical Texts*.

9. The book of Psalms represents a spread from early to late. Job and Ecclesiates are generally considered late. Proverbs and Song of Songs reached their final form late, but they preserve early material. Ruth has characteristics of early and late texts (see Block, *Judges, Ruth*, 590–98).

10. Jastrow, *Dictionary of the Targumim*, 132; Segal, *Grammar of Mishnaic Hebrew*, 42, 141. See also Qimron, *Hebrew of the Dead Sea Scrolls*, 75–76.

7:35; 10:24–25, 35; 19:11; 23:4). This is likely due to the imitation of early biblical Hebrew style.[11]

The Pentateuch and Joshua

The following are examples of the use of the object marker in the Leningrad Codex (*BHS*) of the Pentateuch and Joshua for the preposition אֵת:

לְמוֹעֵד אֲשֶׁר דִּבֶּר אֹתוֹ אֱלֹהִים (Gen 21:2b; LXX αὐτῷ = אִתּוֹ)
at the appointed time that God spoke him (or, with him)

See Gen 34:2, 9 above.[12]

יִשְׁכַּב אִישׁ אֹתָהּ (Lev 15:18, 24; Num 5:13 [*wqtl*]; LXX μετ' αὐτῆς = אִתָּהּ)[13]
a man lies her (or, with her)

לְרִבְעָה אֹתָהּ (Lev 20:16; LXX ὑπ' αὐτοῦ = אִתָּהּ; cf. Lev 18:23)
to lie it (or, with it)

אִם לֹא שָׁכַב אִישׁ אֹתָךְ (Num 5:19; LXX μετὰ σοῦ = אִתָּךְ)[14]
If a man has not lain you (or, with you)

---

11. Morag, "Qumran Hebrew," 150.

12. Compare Gen 34:2b with 2 Sam 13:14b where a few Masoretic manuscripts have עִמָּהּ instead of אֹתָהּ.

13. The Leningrad Codex at Ezek 23:8 has the *plene* spelling אוֹתָהּ with שׁכב, but a multitude of Masoretic manuscripts has the defective spelling אֹתָהּ, which could be vocalized אִתָּהּ.

14. Note the "correct" use of אִתָּךְ earlier in the same verse.

אֲשֶׁר אַתֶּם נִלְחָמִים אוֹתָם (Josh 10:25)[15]
whom you are fighting (or, with whom)

אוּלַי יהוה אוֹתִי (Josh 14:12)[16]
Perhaps the Lord me (or, is with me)

Six of these nine examples have been assigned to the P document (Gen 21:2b; 34:9; Lev 15:18, 24; Num 5:13, 19), the latest pentateuchal source according to the classic expression of the documentary hypothesis. Only Josh 10:25 is without textual variation. The two examples from Joshua involve *plene* spellings, reflecting the practice of later scribes.[17] For the defective spellings, the variation is only in the vocalization.

Samuel and Kings

וַיֶּחֱזַק מִמֶּנָּה וַיְעַנֶּהָ וַיִּשְׁכַּב אֹתָהּ (2 Sam 13:14b; pc Mss עִמָּהּ)
And he was stronger than her and he humbled her and laid her (or, with her)

כִּי קָנוֹ אֶקְנֶה מֵאוֹתְךָ בִּמְחִיר (2 Sam 24:24; mlt Mss מֵאִתְּךָ)
For I will surely purchase from you for a price

וְאַתָּה תִמְנֶה לְךָ חַיִל כַּחַיִל הַנֹּפֵל מֵאוֹתָךְ (1 Kgs 20:25; pc Mss מֵאִתָּךְ)
And you will number for yourself an army like the army that has fallen from you

---

15. The *niphal* of לחם is intransitive and requires a preposition such as בְּ, עִם, or את (but see Ps 109:3). In this example אִתָּם is expected. אוֹתָם also follows *niphal* לחם in 1 Kgs 20:25, but there a few Masoretic manuscripts have אִתָּם. The text of 1 Kgs 20:25 also has מֵאוֹתָךְ, but a few Masoretic manuscripts have מֵאִתָּךְ.

16. The Cairo Geniza and a multitude of Masoretic manuscripts have the spelling אִתִּי. The versions reflect אִתִּי. Cf. Jer 10:5; 20:11.

17. See Andersen and Forbes, *Spelling in the Hebrew Bible*.

A Grammatical Study

וְנִלָּחֲמָה אוֹתָם בַּמִּישׁוֹר (1 Kgs 20:25; pc Mss אִתָּם; cf. Josh 10:25)
And we will fight them (or, with them) in the valley

וְנִדְרְשָׁה מֵאוֹתוֹ (1 Kgs 22:7b; nonn Mss מֵאִתּוֹ; 2 Chr 18:6b מֵאֹתוֹ)
that we might seek from him

עוֹד אִישׁ אֶחָד לִדְרֹשׁ אֶת יְהוָה מֵאוֹתוֹ (1 Kgs 22:8; nonn Mss מֵאִתּוֹ)
There is yet one man to seek the Lord from him
עוֹד אִישׁ אֶחָד לִדְרוֹשׁ אֶת יְהוָה מֵאֹתוֹ (2 Chr 18:7)

אֵי זֶה עָבַר רוּחַ יְהוָה מֵאִתִּי לְדַבֵּר אוֹתָךְ (1 Kgs 22:24b; C אֹתָךְ)
Where did the Spirit of the Lord pass from me to speak you (or, with you)?
אֵי זֶה הַדֶּרֶךְ עָבַר רוּחַ יְהוָה מֵאִתִּי לְדַבֵּר אֹתָךְ (2 Chr 18:23b)

רֵד אוֹתוֹ ... וַיֵּרֶד אוֹתוֹ (2 Kgs 1:15; 2 Mss אִתּוֹ)
"Go down him (or, with him)" ... and he went down him (or, with him)

וְנִדְרְשָׁה אֶת יְהוָה מֵאוֹתוֹ (2 Kgs 3:11; 2 Mss מֵאִתּוֹ; cf. 1 Kgs 22:7b)
that we might seek the Lord from him

יֵשׁ אוֹתוֹ דְּבַר יְהוָה (2 Kgs 3:12; LXX αὐτῷ = אִתּוֹ)
There is him the word of the Lord (or, The word of the Lord is with him)

וַיִּקַּח אוֹתוֹ שְׁבַע מֵאוֹת אִישׁ (2 Kgs 3:26; 2 Mss אִתּוֹ)
And he took him (or, with him) seven hundred men

כִּי רַבִּים אֲשֶׁר אִתָּנוּ מֵאֲשֶׁר אוֹתָם (2 Kgs 6:16b; Ms אִתָּם)
For more are those who are with us than those who are them (or, with them)

85

ודרשת את יהוה מֵאוֹתוֹ (2 Kgs 8:8bα; 2 Mss מֵאִתּוֹ)
and you will seek the Lord from him

In comparison with the occurrences from the Pentateuch, it is apparent that the use of the object marker for the preposition את tends to occur in clusters (Gen 34:2, 9; Lev 15:18, 24; Num 5:13, 19; 1 Kgs 22:7–8, 24; 2 Kgs 3:11–12, 26). Each of the examples from Samuel and Kings involves textual variation. It might be argued that the object marker represents the more difficult reading in each case, but a comparison of 1 Kgs 22:7b (cf. 2 Kgs 3:11) with 2 Chr 18:6b reveals a different process. The Chronicler's source text (מֵאֹתוֹ) represents an earlier form of Kings than that found in the Leningrad Codex.[18] It was incorrectly vocalized at a time when the preposition את fell into widespread disuse, and this led to the incorrect *plene* spelling מֵאוֹתוֹ. Manuscripts representing the MT of 1 Kgs 22:7b have preserved both the *plene* spelling and the reading with the original consonants and vocalization (which were passed down to the Masoretes). The same process can be observed in a comparison of 1 Kgs 22:24b with 2 Chr 18:23b. The misunderstanding and incorrect vocalization (which led to faulty *plene* spellings) of the preposition was not universal or systematic. Thus, correct spellings and vocalizations appear alongside incorrect ones (e.g., 1 Kgs 22:24b; 2 Kgs 6:16b).

Isaiah and Jeremiah

הן גור יגור אפס מֵאוֹתִי (Isa 54:15a; 1QIsa[a] מֵאִתִּי)[19]
If someone stirs up strife, it is not from me

---

[18]. The evidence suggests that the Chronicler had a text of Samuel-Kings that differed from what became the MT (see Abegg et al., *Dead Sea Scrolls Bible*, 260). This evidence primarily comes from a comparison between 4QSam[a] and Chronicles. Of course, there are also disagreements between 4QSam[a] and Chronicles, and the possibility also exists that 4QSam[a] has been corrected on the basis of Chronicles (see Tov, *Greek and Hebrew Bible*, 273–83).

[19]. See מי גר אִתָּךְ in Isa 54:15b.

A Grammatical Study

וְאֲנִי זֹאת בְּרִיתִי אוֹתָם (Isa 59:21; 1QIsa^a אִתָּם; mlt Mss אִתָּם)[20]
And as for me, this is my covenant them (or, with them)

וְדִבַּרְתִּי מִשְׁפָּטַי אוֹתָם (Jer 1:16; mlt Mss אִתָּם)
And I will speak my judgments them (or, with them)

הִנְנִי נִשְׁפָּט אוֹתָךְ (Jer 2:35bα; LXX πρός σέ = אִתָּךְ)
Look, I am entering into judgment you (or, with you)

עַתָּה גַם אֲנִי אֲדַבֵּר מִשְׁפָּטִים אוֹתָם (Jer 4:12b; LXX πρός αὐτούς = אִתָּם)
Now also I will speak judgments them (or, with them)

וַאֲדַבְּרָה אוֹתָם (Jer 5:5; LXX αὐτοῖς = אִתָּם)
and I will speak them (or, with them)

וְגַם הֵיטֵיב אֵין אוֹתָם (Jer 10:5bβ; LXX ἐν αὐτοῖς = אִתָּם)
and also doing good is not them (or, with them)

אַךְ מִשְׁפָּטִים אֲדַבֵּר אוֹתָךְ (Jer 12:1bα; LXX πρός σέ = אִתָּךְ)
but I will speak judgments you (or, with you)

וּבֵית מִשְׁתֶּה לֹא תָבוֹא לָשֶׁבֶת אוֹתָם (Jer 16:8a; nonn Mss אִתָּם)
And a house of feasting you will not enter to sit them (or, with them)

וְשָׁבַרְתָּ הַבַּקְבֻּק לְעֵינֵי הָאֲנָשִׁים הַהֹלְכִים אוֹתָךְ (Jer 19:10; LXX μετά σοῦ = אִתָּךְ)
And you will break the flask to the eyes of the men who are going you (or, with you)

וַיהוָה אוֹתִי כְּגִבּוֹר עָרִיץ (Jer 20:11aα; LXX μετ' ἐμοῦ = אִתִּי)
But the Lord me (or, is with me) like an awe-striking mighty man

---

20. Cf. Gen 17:4a; Ezek 16:8, 60; 37:26.

אוּלִי יַעֲשֶׂה יְהוָה אוֹתָנוּ כְּכָל נִפְלְאֹתָיו (Jer 21:2bα;
אוֹתָנוּ > LXX)
Perhaps the Lord will do us (us > LXX) according to all his wonders

אֲשֶׁר אָנֹכִי עֹשֶׂה אֹתָם (Jer 33:9; אֹתָם > Ms, LXX)[21]
that I am doing them (them > Ms, LXX)

וְדִבַּרְתָּ אוֹתָם (Jer 35:2; > LXX)
and you will speak them (> LXX)

אִתְכֶם? (Jer 38:5b; כִּי אֵין הַמֶּלֶךְ יוּכַל אֶתְכֶם דָּבָר
[LXX: πρὸς αὐτούς = אֹתָם])
For the king is not able to do you (or, with you) a thing

The two examples from Isaiah come from Third Isaiah (post-exilic). It is noteworthy that the oldest complete manuscript of Isaiah, 1QIsaᵃ, preserves the original reading in both cases despite the fact that later books and Qumran manuscripts tend to have fuller spellings.[22] It is unlikely that the *plene* spellings are original, but the appearance of such readings primarily in transitional books reflects the linguistic climate of the period of their later transmission as opposed to the already somewhat established transmission of earlier books. Nearly half (six of thirteen) of the examples from Jeremiah involve the *plene* spelling אוֹתָם. Three of thirteen have אוֹתְךָ. Another three of the examples from Jeremiah use the verb דבר and the object מִשְׁפָּטִים (Jer 1:16; 4:12; 12:1). Three of the last four examples do not appear in the LXX. This last observation is very instructive. The shorter text of LXX Jeremiah generally represents a shorter *Vorlage* and not the work of the translator.[23] Thus, an unnecessary insertion in each case led to misunderstanding, incorrect vocalization, and in two instances incorrect spelling.

21. The end of the verse has אֲשֶׁר אָנֹכִי עֹשֶׂה לָהֶם (Ms לָהֶם).
22. Würthwein, *Text of the OT*, 21–22; Qimron, *Hebrew of the Dead Sea Scrolls*, 17.
23. Tov, *Textual Criticism*, 286–94.

A Grammatical Study

Ezekiel

וַאֲדַבֵּר אוֹתָךְ (Ezek 2:1bβ; LXX πρὸς σέ = אֹתָךְ)[24]
and I will speak you (or, with you)

כִּי סָרָבִים וְסַלּוֹנִים אוֹתָךְ (Ezek 2:6)
for briers (or, rebels?) and thorns you (or, are with you
אֹתָךְ)[25]

וְשָׁם אֲדַבֵּר אוֹתָךְ (Ezek 3:22bβ; LXX πρὸς σέ = אֹתָךְ)
and there I will speak you (or, with you)

וַיְדַבֵּר אֵלַי אֹתִי (Ezek 3:24; LXX πρός με = אִתִּי)
and he spoke me (or, with me)

וּבְדַבְּרִי אוֹתָךְ (Ezek 3:27; LXX πρὸς σέ = אֹתָךְ)
And when I speak you (or, with you)

מִדַּרְכָּם אֶעֱשֶׂה אוֹתָם (Ezek 7:27; LXX αὐτοῖς = אִתָּם)
From (or, according to) their way I will do them (or, with them)

וּבְרוֹמָם יֵרוֹמּוּ אוֹתָם (Ezek 10:17aβ; LXX μετ' αὐτῶν = אִתָּם)
and when they were raised, they were raised them (or, with them)

לָכֵן דַּבֵּר אוֹתָם וְאָמַרְתָּ אֲלֵיהֶם (Ezek 14:4; LXX αὐτοῖς = אִתָּם)
Therefore, speak them (or, with them) and say to them

וָאָבוֹא בִבְרִית אֹתָךְ (Ezek 16:8; LXX μετὰ σοῦ = אִתָּךְ)
and I entered into covenant you (or, with you)

וְעָשִׂיתִי אוֹתָךְ כַּאֲשֶׁר עָשִׂית (Ezek 16:59aβ; LXX ἐν σοί = אִתָּךְ)
And I will do you (or, with you) as you have done

---

24. In Ezek 2:2 the preposition אֶל follows דבר. The *plene* spelling אוֹתָךְ occurs (correctly) in Ezek 2:3–4.

25. See Brown et al., *BDB Hebrew and English Lexicon*, 709.

וזכרתי אני את בריתי אוֹתָךְ בימי נעוריך (Ezek 16:60a; LXX μετὰ σοῦ = אִתָּךְ)
And I will remember my covenant you (or, with you) in the days of your youth

ולא עשיתי אוֹתָם כלה במדבר (Ezek 20:17b; mlt Mss אִתָּם)
and I did not do them (or, with them) complete destruction in the wilderness

לימים אשר אני עשה אוֹתָךְ (Ezek 22:14aβ; mlt Mss אִתָּךְ)
in the days that I do you (or, with you)

כי אוֹתָהּ שכבו בנעוריה (Ezek 23:8; mlt Mss אִתָּהּ)
for they had lain her (or, with her) in her youth

כל בני אשור אוֹתָם (Ezek 23:23aβ; mlt Mss אִתָּם)
all the sons of Assyria them (or, with them)

ועשו אוֹתָךְ בחמה (Ezek 23:25; mlt Mss אִתָּךְ)
and they will do you (or, with you) in wrath

ועשו אוֹתָךְ בשנאה (Ezek 23:29; LXX ἐν σοί = אִתָּךְ)
And they will do you (or, with you) in hatred

ברית עולם יהיה אוֹתָם (Ezek 37:26aβ; mlt Mss אִתָּם; cf. 37:26aα)
An everlasting covenant will be them (or, with them)

אתה וכל אגפיך ועמים רבים אוֹתָךְ (Ezek 38:9b; nonn Mss אִתָּךְ)
you and all your hordes and many peoples you (or, with you)

כטמאתם וכפשעיהם עשיתי אוֹתָם (Ezek 39:24a; LXX αὐτοῖς = אִתָּם)
According to their uncleanness and their transgressions I did them (or, with them)

A Grammatical Study

וּבְאָזְנֶיךָ שְׁמַע אֵת כָּל אֲשֶׁר אֲנִי מְדַבֵּר אֹתָךְ (Ezek 44:5; LXX μετὰ σοῦ = אִתָּךְ)
and in your ears hear all that I am speaking you (or, with you)

The examples from Ezekiel fall into several different groups. Six of twenty-one have the main verb דבר. The *plene* spellings in this group (Ezek 3:22, 27; 14:4) are offset by the original spellings (Ezek 2:1; 3:24; 44:5), which can be vocalized either way. Seven of twenty-one have the main verb עשה. Most of the spellings in this group are *plene* (Ezek 7:27; 16:59; 20:17; 22:14; 23:25, 29), but one (Ezek 39:24) has the original spelling, and most of the others have the original spellings in other Masoretic manuscripts (see also Ezek 20:44). Another group (three of twenty-one) involves the word ברית. Again there is a mix of *plene* (Ezek 16:60; 37:26) and original spellings (Ezek 16:8). The examples in Ezek 2:6; 23:23; 38:9 form another group, leaving only Ezek 10:17; 23:8 without parallels in the book (but see Gen 34:2; Num 5:13, 19; 2 Sam 13:14; 2 Kgs 1:15). Thus, there was a tendency to use the object marker for the preposition את in the same settings. It is probable that use in one influenced use in another of the same kind. It is also noteworthy that the LXX often reflects the original reading in these examples.[26]

Other Examples

וְאֵין אֶתְכֶם אֵלַי נְאֻם יְהוָה (Hag 2:17b)
And there was not you (or, with you אִתְּכֶם?) to me, says the Lord[27]

---

[26]. The LXX of Ezekiel is about four to five percent shorter than MT. "G*-Ezekiel is relatively literal, leading to the assumption that its sequence differences and minuses vis-à-vis M+ reflect a shorter Hebrew parent text. This shorter text was slightly expanded in M+ by various types of elements: exegesis, harmonization, emphasis, parallel words, and new material" (Tov, *Textual Criticism*, 299).

[27]. LXX: καὶ οὐκ ἐπεστρέψατε (= וְלֹא שַׁבְתֶּם).

91

Textuality and the Bible

עַל כֵּן זָחַלְתִּי וָאִירָא מֵחַוֺּת דֵּעִי אֶתְכֶם (Job 32:6b)
Therefore, I withdrew and was afraid of telling you my knowledge (or, declaring my knowledge with you אֶתְכֶם)

Broader Use of אֵת

The suggestion that אֵת is a weakened emphatic particle likely does not explain later use of the object marker for the preposition. It certainly does not explain why the majority of occurrences merely mark the definite direct object without any sense of emphasis.[28] When אֵת marks the grammatical subject of a passive verb (e.g., Gen 4:18), it also marks the object of the verb's action. This use is not far removed from its use as an object marker. But the relatively rare and mostly later use of this particle to mark the subject of an active verb (transitive or intransitive), the subject or predicate of a nominal clause, or the fronted focus/topic of a clause (or *casus pendens*) is probably an extension of the latter (e.g., Neh 9:19, 34).[29] It is perhaps best not to call אֵת the definite direct object marker or an emphatic particle, but a marker whose primary use is to mark the definite direct object.[30] In any case, the broader use

---

28. Wilson, "Particle אֵת in Hebrew," 139-50, 212-24; Kautzsch, *Gesenius' Hebrew Grammar*, 365-66; Kropat, *Syntax des Autors der Chronik*, 2-3, 33-36; Walker, "Concerning the Function of *'t*," 314-15; Saydon, "Meanings of Uses of the Particle אֵת," 192-210; Macdonald, "Particle אֵת in Classical Hebrew," 263-75; Hoftijzer, "Remarks Concerning the Particle *'t*," 1-99; Meyer, "Bemerkungen zur Syntaktischen," 137-42; Waltke and O'Connor, *Introduction to Biblical Hebrew*, 177-79. But see Muraoka, *Emphatic Words and Structures*, 158: "... there is no basis for the assertion that the particle *ēt* can be used for the purpose of emphasis..." Nominal, verbal, prepositional, deictic, and pronominal etymologies have been proposed for the origin of the object marker (see Rubin, *Studies in Semitic Grammaticalization*, 117-27). Hardy has suggested that the marker was originally a demonstrative ("Whence Come Object Markers").

29. Rooker notes that this use became more frequent in Late Biblical Hebrew and Mishnaic Hebrew but that the archaizing tendencies of the Dead Sea Scrolls prevented widespread use in Qumran Hebrew (*Biblical Hebrew in Transition*, 88-90).

30. "... the אֵת seems solely designed to bring the noun into prominence, on the analogy of the אֵת which brings the object into prominence" (Joüon

of the marker אֵת does not seem to include a move in the direction of the preposition אֶת. Thus, it would be a stretch to explain the examples above purely on the basis of a development in the use of the object marker.³¹ It is more likely that a decline in usage of the preposition אֶת led to misunderstanding and misuse, which tended to cluster and repeat in certain constructions.

Conclusion

The object marker for the preposition אֶת occurs primarily in books that represent Hebrew in transition (Kings, Jeremiah, Ezekiel). This phenomenon tends to occur in specific groupings (e.g., clusters within passages, usage with a very limited number of verbs), perhaps due to a kind of chain reaction in which one occurrence of each kind influenced others of the same kind. The influence of Aramaic (which prefers עִם) led to the increasing disuse of the preposition in later biblical Hebrew (Esther, Ezra, Daniel, Chronicles). This in turn led to sporadic misunderstanding of the preposition by those who were not familiar with it, which in transmission of texts not well established resulted in vocalization of אֵת as the more familiar object marker.³² This incorrect vocalization then led to incorrect *plene* spellings. But the original spelling and correct vocalization are often preserved in the textual witnesses. No explanation of the phenomenon from the broader use of אֵת seems to be plausible.³³

---

and Muraoka, *Grammar of Biblical Hebrew*, 417). See Shepherd, "So-called Emphasis," 193.

31. Aquila's use of σύν to render the object marker was driven by a concern to represent each part of the Hebrew text in a literalistic manner (Tov, *Textual Criticism*, 144). This included those parts of the text that had no direct equivalent in the target language.

32. The vocalization of the object marker and the preposition is the same without pronominal suffixes. It was thus an easy move to make the vocalization with suffixes identical.

33. This chapter was originally presented at the 2012 NAPH International Conference on Hebrew Language, Literature, and Culture (June 25–27), which was held at the University of California, Los Angeles.

7

A Study in Semantics
אהב "Choose"

A NUMBER OF LEXICONS, commentaries, and translations recognize the meaning "reject" in the semantic range of the biblical Hebrew root שנא ("hate").[1] It is not difficult to find examples in the biblical corpus where the root likely has this sense.[2] For instance, there is no indication from the context that Jacob "hated" Leah (Gen 29:31, 33). It was simply the case that she was not the preferred of the two wives (Deut 21:15–17). Thus, שנא can be the opposite of בחר ("choose") in the parallelism of Prov 1:29: "Because they reject (שנא) knowledge, and they do not choose (בחר) the fear of YHWH."

It is surprising then that the same lexicons, commentaries, and translations generally do not acknowledge the corresponding meaning "choose" in the semantic range of the antonym אהב ("love"). And yet there are numerous occurrences where the gloss "love" does not fit the context. For example, Gen 25:28 indicates which children (Esau or Jacob) were preferred or favored by their parents (Isaac and Rebekah). It does not imply that the parents only loved one of the children and hated the other. The two parents

---

1. E.g., Bullinger, *Figures of Speech*, 556; *TLOT* 2:653; *DCH* 8:167–72.

2. Gen 26:27; 29:31, 33; Exod 18:21; 20:5; Deut 5:9; 7:10; 21:15, 16, 17; 22:13, 16; 24:3; Judg 11:7; 15:2; 2 Sam 19:7; Isa 1:14; 60:15; 66:5; Jer 12:8; Ezek 35:6; Hos 9:15; Amos 5:15, 21; Mic 3:2; Mal 1:3; Pss 5:6; 11:5; 26:5; 31:7; 50:17; 97:10; 101:3; 119:104, 113, 128, 163; Job 8:22; Prov 1:22, 29; 5:12; 8:13, 36; 11:15; 12:1; 13:5; 15:10, 27; 19:17; 28:16; 30:23.

A Study in Semantics

merely had their respective preferences, which naturally led to their unintended neglect of the child they did not choose.

The thesis of this chapter is that the meaning "choose" for אהב is well founded and common enough to be included in the standard lexicons. This will require demonstration of this meaning from usage. The translation equivalent "love" does not cover the full semantic range of אהב. Furthermore, the range of the English term "love" has meanings and connotations that do not correspond exactly to the Hebrew אהב. It will also be necessary to place אהב within the semantic field of "choice" and ask why a language user would employ אהב rather than בחר. This will lead to a more complete definition of these terms. It will also prove helpful to track the corresponding use of the antonym שנא and its relationship to other words in the same field of meaning (e.g., מאס, זנח).

Usage of אהב

It is conceded here that all the usual and widely recognized meanings of אהב are present in the Hebrew Bible: marital love (Gen 24:67; Judg 14:16; 16:15; Hos 3:1; Eccl 9:9), love of food (Gen 27:4, 9, 14), lust (Gen 34:3; Judg 16:4; 2 Sam 13:1, 4, 15; 1 Kgs 11:1-2; Hos 3:1), love of neighbor (Lev 19:18, 34; Deut 10:19), loyal devotion to God (Deut 6:5; 10:12; 11:1, 13, 22; 13:4; 19:9; 30:6, 16, 20; Josh 22:5; 23:11; 1 Kgs 3:3; Mic 6:8; Pss 5:12; 31:24; 69:37; 116:1; 119:32; 145:20; 1QS 1:3-4), God's loyal devotion to his people (Deut 7:13; 10:18; Isa 43:4; 56:6; 63:9; Jer 2:2; 31:3; Hos 11:4; Zeph 3:17; Ps 146:8; Prov 15:9; Dan 9:4; Neh 1:5), fondness/adoration (1 Sam 16:21; 18:1, 16, 20, 22, 28; 20:17; 2 Sam 1:23; Song 1:3, 4), friendship/alliance (1 Kgs 5:1; Isa 48:14; Jer 20:4, 6; 22:20, 22; 30:14; Zech 13:6; Pss 38:12; 88:19; 109:4, 5; Job 19:19; Prov 17:9, 17; 18:24; 27:6; Esth 5:10, 14; 6:13), love of enemies (2 Sam 19:7), love of bribes (Isa 1:23), love of deception (Hos 12:8; Zech 8:17), love of sleep (Isa 56:10; Prov 20:13), love of idols (Isa 57:8; Jer 2:25; 8:2; Hos 9:10), love of justice (Isa 61:8; Pss 33:5; 37:28; 45:8; 99:4; Prov 16:13), love of Jerusalem (Isa 66:10; Ps 122:6), sexual love in metaphor (Ezek 16:33, 36, 37; 23:5, 9, 22; Hos 2:7, 9, 12, 14, 15; Lam

1:2, 19), love to thresh grain (Hos 10:11), love to display offerings (Amos 4:5), love of truth and peace (Zech 8:19), love of holy things (Mal 2:11), love of emptiness (Ps 4:3), love of violence (Ps 11:5), love of uprightness (Ps 11:7), love for the temple (Ps 26:8), love of days (Ps 34:13), love of salvation (Pss 40:17; 70:5), love of curse, love of commands/torah (Pss 119:47, 48, 97, 113, 119, 127, 140, 159, 163, 165, 167), YHWH/parent disciplines those he loves (Prov 3:12; 13:24), appreciation for a rebuke (Prov 9:8; 15:12), love of the rich, love of the tongue (Prov 18:21), love of self (1 Sam 20:17; Prov 19:8), love of joy/wine/oil (Prov 21:17), love for the pure of heart (Prov 22:11), devotion (Ruth 4:15), the love between two lovers (2 Sam 1:26; Prov 5:19; Song 1:7; 2:4, 5; 3:1–4; 5:8; 8:6, 7), time to love (Eccl 3:8), love of money (Eccl 5:9), love of the land (2 Chr 26:10), human love (Prov 10:12; 15:17; 27:5; Eccl 9:1, 6), love personified (Song 2:7; 3:5, 10; 7:7; 8:4), and adulterous love (Jer 2:33).

Likewise there is no reason to dispute the accepted semantic range of שנא: hatred (Gen 37:4, 5, 8; Lev 19:17; Num 35:20; Deut 1:27; 4:42; 9:28; 12:31; 16:22; 19:4, 6, 11; Josh 20:5; Judg 14:16; 2 Sam 13:15, 22; 1 Kgs 22:8; Isa 61:8; Jer 44:4; Ezek 16:37; 23:29; 35:11; Amos 5:10; 6:8; Zech 8:17; Mal 2:16; Pss 25:19; 34:22; 36:3; 45:8; 105:25; 109:3, 5; 120:6; 129:5; 139:21, 22; Job 34:17; Prov 6:16; 9:8; 10:12, 18; 13:24; 14:17, 20; 15:17; 25:17; 26:24, 26, 28; 29:10; Eccl 2:17, 18; 3:8; 9:1, 6; 2 Chr 18:7; CD 2:13, 15; 1QS 1:4; 11QT 65:7, 11), and enemy (Gen 24:60; Exod 1:10; 23:5; Lev 26:17; Num 10:35; Deut 7:15; 30:7; 32:41; 33:11; 2 Sam 5:8; 22:18, 41; Ezek 16:27; 23:28; Pss 9:14; 18:18, 41; 21:9; 25:19; 35:19; 38:20; 41:8; 44:8, 11; 55:13; 68:2; 69:5, 15; 81:16; 83:3; 86:17; 89:24; 106:10, 41; 118:7; 139:22; Job 31:29; Prov 25:21; 27:6; 29:24; Esth 9:1, 5, 16; 2 Chr 1:11; 19:2).[3]

In the canonical arrangement of the Tanakh, the first use of אהב where the meaning "choose" is likely is in Gen 22:2: "And he said, 'Take your son, your only son whom you prefer (אהבת), Isaac . . .'" It would not be appropriate in this context to call Isaac the only son loved by Abraham (see *Tg. Ps.-J.* Gen 22:1; *b. Sanh.* 89b). Isaac is the only son born by Sarah, but it is clear from texts

---

3. See Anderson, "Enemies and Evil-doers," 18–29.

A Study in Semantics

like Gen 17:18; 21:11 that Abraham also cares for Ishmael. It is simply the case that Isaac is the chosen son (Gen 17:21; 21:12). It is possible then that a Semitic original is behind the textual variation of Luke 9:35: (1) ὁ υἱός μου ὁ ἐκλελεγμένος ("my son, the chosen") or (2) ὁ υἱός μου ὁ ἀγαπητός ("my son, the beloved") (cf. Matt 3:17; 17:5; Mark 1:11; 9:7; Luke 3:22). These would be two different interpretations of the same original rather than two separate renderings of different originals.

The use of אהב in Gen 25:28 has already been mentioned above as an example of parental preference for a child rather than exclusive love. A similar example is Jacob's preference for Joseph (Gen 37:3-4) and then his preference for Benjamin after the death of Joseph (Gen 44:20).[4] Mention has also been made of the use of שנא in Gen 29:31, 33, where Leah is not the hated wife but the neglected wife. The converse of this is that Rachel is the chosen or preferred wife (Deut 21:15-17): "And Jacob preferred (ויאהב) Rachel" (Gen 29:18a). This is what is said directly after the contrast of the physical appearances of Rachel and Leah in Gen 29:17. Jacob's seven years of work for Rachel seemed like a few days precisely because he had made his choice and knew exactly for whom he was working (Gen 29:20). Jacob's preference for Rachel was not a hatred of Leah (Gen 29:30).[5] In fact, Leah hoped to win Jacob's favor through her childbearing (Gen 29:32). Another example of a preferred wife is Hannah: "It was Hannah whom he preferred (אהב)" (1 Sam 1:5b). Like Rachel, Hannah was preferred even though she was the barren one.

---

4. "And Israel, he preferred (אהב) Joseph more than/apart from all his sons ... And his brothers saw that it was him whom their father preferred (אהב) more than/apart from all his brothers, and they rejected (וישנאו) him ..." (Gen 37:3-4). "And we said to my lord, 'We have an old father and a small lad born in his old age, and it was his brother who died, and he alone was left to his mother, and as for his father, he favors him (אהבו)'" (Gen 44:20).

5. The use of מן in this verse to mean "more than" or perhaps "apart from" is similar to its use in 2 Chr 11:21: "And Rehoboam preferred (ויאהב) Maacah the daughter of Absalom more than (מכל) all his wives and concubines..." This does not mean that Rehoboam loved Maacah and hated the others. It means that Maacah was his preference or choice above all the others.

The occurrence of אהב in the Decalogue (Exod 20:6; Deut 5:10; 7:9; cf. Judg 5:31) likely means "choose," but its use is similar to that in Deuteronomy where it means covenant loyalty or devotion to God. This is in contrast to those who reject (שׂנא) God (Exod 20:5; Deut 5:9). In the Covenant Code, אהב is used when a servant has to make a choice between his family and his freedom: "And if indeed the servant says, 'I choose (אהבתי) my master, my wife, and my sons, I will not go out free'" (Exod 21:5; cf. Deut 15:16). It is not a question of whether or not the servant loves freedom. It is a decision that must be made between two options.

Several texts in Deuteronomy put אהב together with בחר ("choose"):

> And because he chose (אהב) your fathers, he elected (ויבחר) their seed after them and brought you by his presence, by his great strength out of Egypt (Deut 4:37).

> Not because of your greatness more than all the peoples was YHWH attached (חשׁק) to you and did he elect (ויבחר) you. For you are the least of all the peoples. But because YHWH chose (מאהבת) you and kept the oath that he swore to your fathers, YHWH brought you out with a strong hand and purchased you from the house of servitude, from the hand of Pharaoh the king of Egypt (Deut 7:7–8; cf. Deut 23:6).

> Only it was to your fathers that YHWH was attached (חשׁק) in choosing (לאהבה) them,[6] and he elected (ויבחר) their seed after them, you from all the peoples as this day (Deut 10:15).

It could be argued that Deut 4:37 means that because God loved the fathers so much he elected their descendants. But this overlooks the use of election terminology with reference to the fathers (Josh 24:3; Pss 105:6; 135:4; Neh 9:7). The election of the fathers included the election of their offspring (Gen 12:1–3, 7). It also overlooks the fact that divine election was not based on merit. This is the point of Deut 7:7–8. This is also the point of Deut 9:5–6. Furthermore,

---

6. For this use of the infinitive construct, see GKC §114o.

A Study in Semantics

אהב and בחר appear to be almost interchangeable in Deut 4:37 and Deut 7:7-8. In Deut 4:37, the fathers are the object of אהב, and their seed is the object of בחר. But in Deut 7:7-8, their seed is the object of בחר and אהב. What then is the difference between אהב and בחר? Is the use of two different words for "choose" simply a stylistic preference? It may very well be that the use of חשק in Deut 7:7-8 and 10:15 is the clue. It was in choosing (אהב) the fathers that YHWH was attached (חשק) to them. That is, while בחר has the more generic sense of "choose" or "elect," אהב carries the more specific nuance of devotion or commitment (see 1 Kgs 10:9; Jer 31:3; Hos 3:1; 2 Chr 2:10; 9:8). It is then possible also to suggest that this is what creates the distinction between שנא and מאס. מאס has the general meaning "reject." שנא has the specific sense of detachment from a commitment.

According to 2 Sam 12:24 (cf. Neh 13:26), YHWH "loved" (אהב) Solomon. Therefore, the prophet Nathan named him Jedidiah, "the beloved of YHWH" (2 Sam 12:25; cf. Isa 5:1). It would seem, however, that the sense in which the subsequent narrative understands this is that YHWH elected Solomon to be David's successor. The next reference to Solomon is in 1 Kgs 1:13: "Did not you, my lord the king, swear to your maidservant, saying, 'Solomon your son will be king after me, and he will sit on my throne'?" These words, which Nathan advised Bathsheba to say to David in his old age, presuppose that David had chosen Solomon to be his successor, yet the only account of this is in 1 Chronicles 22-29 where David makes extensive preparations for Solomon before his death. The only possible antecedent for 1 Kgs 1:13 in the Former Prophets is 2 Sam 12:24.

The text of Isa 41:8 provides another example where אהב occurs with election terminology:

> But you, Israel, my servant,
> Jacob, whom I have chosen (בחרתי),
> seed of Abraham, my friend (אהבי)

There is some doubt about whether "my friend" modifies "Abraham" or the "seed of Abraham" (cf. 2 Chr 20:7).[7] The descriptions "my servant" and "whom I have chosen" in the first two lines modify the nation of Israel/Jacob. The reader might then expect "my friend" in the third line to describe the "seed of Abraham." On the other hand, Jas 2:23 takes "Abraham" to be "the friend of God." Of course, both Abraham (Neh 9:7) and the seed of Abraham (Ezek 20:5) are "chosen" (בחר) (see also Ps 47:5 [אהב//בחר]). A similar difficulty arises in Ps 105:6 and creates textual variation:

L	The seed of Abraham, his servant (עבדו),	
	The sons of Jacob, his chosen ones (בחיריו)	
11QPsa	The seed of Abraham, his servants (עבדיו),	
	The sons of Jacob, his chosen one (בחירו)	

Both versions of the text are mixed, but in different ways. Presumably in the original text both words placed in apposition were either singular or plural. In the course of transmission there was a change from one to the other and then conflation of the two.

The prophets speak of the choices or preferences of the people using אהב. According to Jer 5:31, when the prophets prophesy falsely, the people "like it" (אהבו) that way. They "prefer" (אהבו) to wander (Jer 14:10). According to Hosea, Israel has chosen harlotry over faithfulness to YHWH (Hos 4:18; 9:1). These are not references to an emotion or feeling of love for what is false. It is a conscious choice that the people are making. Therefore, the Lord "rejects" (שׂנא) them and no longer "chooses" (אהב) them (Hos 9:15). He will one day "choose" (אהב) them again (Hos 14:5) as he once did (Hos 11:1), but they must "reject" (שׂנא) evil and "choose" (אהב) good (Amos 5:15; cf. Mic 3:2; 6:8; Pss 52:5, 6; 97:10).

---

7. It is likely that the proposed vocalization אֹהֲבִי is to be preferred to אֹהֲבִי. See the Greek versions of Isa 41:8; 2 Chr 20:7. Verse 9 of Isaiah 41 stresses God's election, not Abraham's love of God (see Westermann, *Isaiah 40–66*, 70).

A Study in Semantics

The opening disputation of Mal 1:2-5 offers a particularly telling example with a web of intertextual links:

> "I chose (אהבתי) you," says YHWH.
> And you will say, "How did you choose us (אהבתנו)?"
> "Was not Esau Jacob's brother?" says YHWH.
> "And I chose (ואהב) Jacob, but Esau I rejected (שנאתי)."

This is first of all a reading of Gen 25:19-34; 26:34-35; 27:27-29, 39-40, 46; 28:8-9. Before Esau and Jacob were even born, the election of Jacob was determined (Gen 25:23). This then had direct implications for the nations that came from the two sons of Isaac. Just as Rebekah "preferred" (אהבת) Jacob to Esau (Gen 25:28b), so YHWH "chose" Jacob (Mal 1:2). The apostle makes the point from Genesis and Malachi that election, whether individual or corporate, is by grace and not by works (Rom 9:10-18).

The election of Zion is cast in terms of אהב:

> And he elected (ויבחר) the tribe of Judah,
> Mount Zion, which he chose (אהב) (Ps 78:68).

This is in contrast to the rejection (מאס) of the tent of Joseph, the tribe of Ephraim (Ps 78:68).

> YHWH prefers (אהב) the gates of Zion to all the dwellings of Jacob (Ps 87:2).

In the book of Proverbs, there is often a choice to be made between wisdom and folly:

> "How long will you simpletons choose (תאהבו) simplicity,
> And scoffers prefer (חמדו) scoffing for themselves,
> And fools reject (ישנאו) knowledge?" (Prov 1:22)
> "All those who reject me (משנאי) choose (אהבו) death."
> (Prov 8:36b)
> He who accepts (אהב) discipline chooses (אהב) knowledge,
> But he who rejects (שנא) correction is a brute. (Prov 12:1)

These texts do not speak of an emotional attachment but a decision. See also Prov 4:6; 8:17, 21; 17:19; 29:3.

Finally, the book of Esther says that king Ahasuerus "preferred" (וַיֶּאֱהַב) Esther to all the other women (Esth 2:17). This is because she proved to be "better than" queen Vashti (Esth 1:19).

Semantic Field of אהב

Just as one part of the semantic range of שנא falls within the semantic field of "rejection" (מאס), so one part of the semantic range of אהב falls within the semantic field of "choice" (בחר). The use of אהב instead of בחר (or שנא instead of מאס) can be a stylistic preference. For example, in a parallelistic line it is stylistically preferable to use two synonyms rather than repetition of the same word. At other times, however, אהב can have a specific nuance that בחר does not carry. אהב is used with the meaning "choose" when the writer wants to include the sense of devotion or commitment. This does not mean that commitment is necessarily absent in the act referred to by בחר. It is only to say that this is not part of the semantic content that בחר brings to a context. Likewise שנא carries a sense of detachment that מאס does not.

Conclusion

Given the appropriate context, אהב can mean "to choose with devotion or commitment." Likewise שנא can mean "to reject by detachment." In particular, it is to be noted that אהב in descriptions of divine-human relationships does not indicate a feeling. This is not to say that feelings are absent from the relationship to which אהב refers. It is simply to say that אהב speaks of an act of devotion. This is also noteworthy when seen in continuity with New Testament teaching on ἀγάπη as a specific act that serves as the basis of the covenant relationship (John 3:16; Rom 5:9; Eph 2:4; 1 John 4:9–10).

Bibliography

Abegg, Martin Jr., et al. *The Dead Sea Scrolls Bible.* San Francisco: Harper, 1999.
Alter, Robert. *The Art of Biblical Narrative.* Rev ed. New York: Basic, 2011.
Andersen, Francis I., and A. Dean Forbes. *Spelling in the Hebrew Bible.* Rome: Biblical Institute Press, 1986.
Anderson, G. W. "Enemies and Evil-doers in the Book of Psalms." *Bulletin of the John Rylands University Library of Manchester* 48 (1965-66) 18-29.
Bar-Efrat, Shimon. *Narrative Art in the Bible.* London: T & T Clark, 2004.
Barr, James. *Comparative Philology and the Text of the Old Testament.* Oxford: Oxford University Press, 1968. Reprint with additions and corrections, Winona Lake, IN: Eisenbrauns, 1987.
———. *The Semantics of Biblical Language.* Oxford: Oxford University Press, 1961.
Barth, Karl. *Church Dogmatics.* Vol. 1.2. Edinburgh: T & T Clark, 1958.
Barthélemy, D. *Les Devanciers d'Aquila.* Leiden, NLD: Brill, 1963.
———. "La Qualité du Texte Massorétique de Samuel." In *The Hebrew and Greek Texts of Samuel,* edited by E. Tov, 1-44. Jerusalem: Academon, 1980.
Baumgartner, A. J. Étude *Critique sur l'état du Texte du Livre des Proverbes d'après les Principales Traductions Anciennes.* Leipzig: Drugulin, 1890.
Berlin, Adele. *Poetics and Interpretation of Biblical Narrative.* Winona Lake, IN: Eisenbrauns, 1994.
Blenkinsopp, Joseph. *Prophecy and Canon: A Contribution to the Study of Jewish Origins.* Notre Dame: University of Notre Dame Press, 1977.
Block, Daniel I. *Judges, Ruth.* New American Commentary. Nashville: Broadman & Holman, 1999.
Brown, Francis, et al. *The Brown-Driver-Briggs Hebrew and English Lexicon.* Boston: Houghton, Mifflin, & Co., 1906. Reprint, Peabody, MA: Hendrickson, 2001.
Büchler, A. "Zur Geschichte der Tempelmusik und der Tempelpsalmen." *Zeitschrift für die alttestamentliche Wissenschaft* (1899) 109-14.
Budde, K. *Die Bücher Richter und Samuel.* Giessen, DEU: J. Ricker, 1890.
Bullinger, E. W. *Figures of Speech Used in the Bible.* London: Eyre & Spottiswoode, 1898. Reprint, Grand Rapids: Baker, 1968.

Bibliography

Busch, Eberhard. *Karl Barth: His Life from Letters and Autobiographical Texts*. Translated by John Bowden. London: SCM, 1976. Reprint, Eugene, OR: Wipf & Stock, 2005.

Carr, David. *The Formation of the Hebrew Bible: A New Reconstruction*. Oxford: Oxford University Press, 2011.

Carson, D. A. "Syntactical and Text-Critical Observations on John 20:30–31: One More Round on the Purpose of the Fourth Gospel." *Journal of Biblical Literature* 124 (2005) 693–714.

Chapman, Stephen B. *The Law and the Prophets*. Forschungen zum Alten Testament 27. Tübingen: Mohr Siebeck, 2000.

Childs, Brevard S. *Biblical Theology of the Old and New Testaments: Theological Reflection on the Christian Bible*. Minneapolis: Fortress, 1992.

Christensen, Duane L. "Num 21:14–15 and the Book of the Wars of Yahweh." *Catholic Biblical Quarterly* 36 (1974) 359–60.

Clines, David J. A. *The Dictionary of Classical Hebrew*. Sheffield, ENG: Sheffield Phoenix, 2011.

Curtis, Edward Lewis, and Albert Alonzo Madsen. *A Critical and Exegetical Commentary on the Books of Chronicles*. International Critical Commentary. New York: Charles Scribner's Sons, 1910.

Davies, Philip R., and Thomas Römer, eds. *Writing the Bible: Scribes, Scribalism, and Script*. Durham: Acumen, 2013.

Delekat, L. "Die Peschitta zu Jesaja zwischen Targum und Septuaginta." *Biblica* 38 (1957) 185–99, 321–35.

———. "Ein Septuagintatargum." *Vetus Testamentum* 8 (1958) 225–52.

Diringer, David. "The Biblical Scripts." In *The Cambridge History of the Bible*, vol. 1, *From the Beginnings to Jerome*, edited by P. R. Ackroyd and C. F. Evans, 11–29. Cambridge: Cambridge University Press, 1970.

Dirksen, Peter B. "The Old Testament Peshitta." In *Mikra: Text, Translation, Reading & Interpretation of the Hebrew Bible in Ancient Judaism & Early Christianity*, edited by Martin Jan Mulder and Harry Sysling, 255–97. Philadelphia: Fortress, 1988. Reprint, Peabody, MA: Hendrickson, 2004.

Driver, S. R. *An Introduction to the Literature of the Old Testament*. New York: Charles Scribner's Sons, 1891.

———. *Notes on the Hebrew Text and the Topography of the Books of Samuel*. 2nd ed. Oxford: Oxford University Press, 1912. Reprint, Eugene, OR: Wipf & Stock, 2004.

Ernesti, J. A. *Institutio interpretis Novi Testamenti*. 3rd ed. Leipzig: Weidmann & Reich, 1774.

Fishbane, Michael. *Biblical Interpretation in Ancient Israel*. Oxford: Clarendon, 1985.

Fokkelman, J. P. *Reading Biblical Narrative: An Introductory Guide*. Translated by Ineke Smit. Louisville: Westminster John Knox, 1999.

Freedman, David Noel. "Pottery, Poetry, and Prophecy: An Essay on Biblical Poetry." *Journal of Biblical Literature* 96 (1977) 5–26.

Bibliography

Frei, Hans W. *The Eclipse of Biblical Narrative: A Study in Eighteenth and Nineteenth Century Hermeneutics.* New Haven, CT: Yale University Press, 1974.

Gunkel, Hermann, and Joachim Begrich. *An Introduction to the Psalms: The Genres of the Religious Lyric of Israel.* Translated by James D. Nogalski. Macon, GA: Mercer University Press, 1998.

Habel, N. C. *Literary Criticism of the Old Testament.* Philadelphia: Fortress, 1971.

Hardy, Humphrey. "Whence Come Object Markers in Northwest Semitic?" Paper, North American Conference on Afroasiatic Linguistics 37. Albuquerque, NM, March 2009.

Hoftijzer, J. "Remarks Concerning the Use of the Particle *'t* in Classical Hebrew." *Oudtestamentische Studiën* 14 (1965) 1–99.

Holladay, William L. *Jeremiah 2: A Commentary on the Book of the Prophet Jeremiah Chapters 26–52.* Hermeneia. Minneapolis: Fortress, 1989.

Jastrow, Marcus. *Dictionary of the Targumim, Talmud Babli, Yerushalmi, and Midrashic Literature.* Reprint, New York: Judaica, 1996.

Jenni, Ernst, and Claus Westermann, eds. *Theological Lexicon of the Old Testament.* Vol. 1. Translated by Mark E. Biddle. Peabody, MA: Hendrickson, 1997.

Johnson, B. *Die Hexaplarische Rezension des 1 Samuelbuches der Septuaginta.* Lund: C.W.K. Gleerup, 1963.

Joüon, Paul, and Takamitsu Muraoka. *A Grammar of Biblical Hebrew.* 2nd ed. Rome: Gregorian and Biblical, 2009.

Kahle, Paul E. *The Cairo Geniza.* 2nd ed. New York: Praeger, 1960.

Kautzsch, E., ed. *Gesenius' Hebrew Grammar.* 28th ed. Translated by A. E. Cowley, 2nd English ed. Oxford: Clarendon, 1910.

Klein, Ralph W. *1 Chronicles.* Hermeneia. Minneapolis: Fortress, 2006.

———. *2 Chronicles.* Hermeneia. Minneapolis: Fortress, 2012.

Koehler, Ludwig, and Walter Baumgartner. *The Hebrew and Aramaic Lexicon of the Old Testament.* Leiden, NLD: Brill, 2001.

Kropat, Arno. *Die Syntax des Autors der Chronik verglichen mit der seiner Quellen: Ein Beitrag zur historischen Syntax des Hebräischen.* BZAW 16. Giessen, DEU: Töppelmann, 1909.

Kuenen, A. *Historisch-kritische Einleitung in die Bücher des Alten Testaments.* Vol. 1, pt. 2. Leipzig: Otto Schulze, 1890.

Levine, Etan. *The Aramaic Version of the Bible.* Berlin: de Gruyter, 1988.

Lilly, Ingrid E. *The Two Books of Ezekiel: Papyrus 967 and the Masoretic Text as Variant Literary Editions.* Leiden, NLD: Brill, 2012.

Lindbeck, George A. *The Nature of Doctrine: Religion and Theology in a Postliberal Age.* Philadelphia: Westminster, 1984.

Longman, Tremper. *Song of Songs.* New International Commentary on the Old Testament. Grand Rapids: Eerdmans, 2001.

Longman, Tremper, and Raymond B. Dillard. *An Introduction to the Old Testament.* 2nd ed. Grand Rapids: Zondervan, 2006.

Bibliography

Lund, J. A. "The Influence of the Septuagint on the Peshitta: A Re-evaluation of Criteria in Light of Comparative Study of the Versions in Genesis and Psalms." PhD diss., Hebrew University, Jerusalem, 1988.

Macdonald, John. "The Particle את in Classical Hebrew." *Vetus Testamentum* 14 (1964) 263–75.

Martin, Gary D. *Multiple Originals: New Approaches to Hebrew Bible Textual Criticism*. Atlanta: SBL, 2010.

McCarter, P. *1 Samuel*. Anchor Bible. New York: Doubleday, 1980.

McConville, J. G. *Deuteronomy*. Downers Grove, IL: InterVarsity, 2002.

Meyer, R. "Bemerkungen zur Syntaktischen Funktion der sogenannten Nota Accusativi." In *Wort and Geschichte: Festschrift für Karl Elliger*, edited by H. Gese and H. P. Rüger, 137–42. Kevelaer, DEU: Butzon & Bercker, 1973.

Miller-Naudé, Cynthia, and Ziony Zevit, eds. *Diachrony in Biblical Hebrew*. LSAWS 8. Winona Lake, IN: Eisenbrauns, 2012.

Morag, Shelomo. "Qumran Hebrew: Some Typological Observations." *Vetus Testamentum* 38 (1988) 148–64.

———. "The Tiberian Tradition of Biblical Hebrew: Homogeneity and Heterogeneity." (Heb.) In *The Annual of the Shocken Institute for Jewish Studies* 2, 105–44. Jerusalem: Magnes, 1974.

Muraoka, Takamitsu. *Emphatic Words and Structures in Biblical Hebrew*. Jerusalem: Magnes, 1985.

Naudé, Jacobus A. "Linguistic Dating of Biblical Hebrew Texts: The Chronology and Typology Debate." *Journal of Northwest Semitic Languages* 36 (2010) 1–22.

Neusner, Jacob. *Introduction to Rabbinic Literature*. New York: Doubleday, 1994.

Noth, Martin. *The Deuteronomistic History*. Sheffield, ENG: JSOT, 1981.

Peters, Norbert. *Beiträge zur Text- und Literarkritik sowie zur Erklärung der Bücher Samuel*. Freiburg im Breisgau: Herder, 1899.

Petersen, David L. *Late Israelite Prophecy: Studies in Deutero-Prophetic Literature and in Chronicles*. SBLMS 23. Missoula, MT: Scholars, 1977.

Pritchard, James B., ed. *Ancient Near Eastern Texts Relating to the Old Testament*. 3rd ed. Princeton: Princeton University Press, 1969.

Qimron, Elisha. *The Hebrew of the Dead Sea Scrolls*. Reprint, Winona Lake, IN: Eisenbrauns, 2008.

Rendtorff, Rolf. *The Canonical Hebrew Bible: A Theology of the Old Testament*. Translated by David E. Orton. Leiden, NLD: Deo, 2005.

———. "Zur Komposition des Buches Jesaja." *Vetus Testamentum* 34 (1984) 295–320.

Reventlow, Henning Graf. *History of Biblical Interpretation*. Vol. 3, *Renaissance, Reformation, Humanism*. Translated by James O. Duke. Atlanta: SBL, 2010.

Rollston, Christopher A. *Writing and Literacy in the World of Ancient Israel: Epigraphic Evidence from the Iron Age*. Atlanta: SBL, 2010.

Rooker, Mark F. *Biblical Hebrew in Transition: The Language of the Book of Ezekiel*. Sheffield, ENG: JSOT, 1990.

Bibliography

Rubin, A. *Studies in Semitic Grammaticalization*. Winona Lake, IN: Eisenbrauns, 2005.
Sailhamer, John H. *Introduction to Old Testament Theology*. Grand Rapids: Zondervan, 1995.
———. *The Meaning of the Pentateuch: Revelation, Composition, and Interpretation*. Downers Grove, IL: InterVarsity, 2009.
———. *The Pentateuch as Narrative*. Grand Rapids: Zondervan, 1992.
Saussure, Ferdinand de. *Cours de Linguistique Générale*. Edited by Charles Bally and Albert Sechehaye. Paris: Payothèque, 1916.
Saydon, P. P. "Meanings of Uses of the Particle את." *Vetus Testamentum* 14 (1964) 192–210.
Schmid, J. *Septuagintageschichtliche Studien zum 1. Samuelbuch*. Breslau, 1941.
Schmidt, Brian B., ed. *Contextualizing Israel's Sacred Writings: Ancient Literacy, Orality, and Literary Production*. Atlanta: SBL, 2015.
Schmitt, Hans-Christoph. "Redaktion des Pentateuch im Geiste der Prophetie." *Vetus Testamentum* 32 (1982) 170–89.
Schniedewind, William M. *How the Bible Became a Book*. Cambridge: Cambridge University Press, 2004.
Segal, M. H. *A Grammar of Mishnaic Hebrew*. Oxford: Clarendon, 1927. Reprint, Eugene, OR: Wipf & Stock, 2001.
Seitz, Christopher R. *Prophecy and Hermeneutics: Toward a New Introduction to the Prophets*. Grand Rapids: Baker, 2007.
———. "Two Testaments and the Failure of One Tradition History." In *Biblical Theology: Retrospect and Prospect*, edited by Scott J. Hafemann, 195–211. Downers Grove, IL: InterVarsity, 2002.
Shepherd, Michael B. "Compositional Analysis of the Twelve." *Zeitschrift für die alttestamentliche Wissenschaft* 120 (2008) 184–93.
———. *Daniel in the Context of the Hebrew Bible*. New York: Peter Lang, 2009.
———. "Hebrew Acrostic Poems and Their Vocabulary Stock." *Journal of Northwest Semitic Languages* 36 (2010) 95–108.
———. "The New Exodus in the Composition of the Twelve." In *Text and Canon*, edited by Paul Kissling and Robert Cole. Eugene, OR: Pickwick, forthcoming.
———. "So-called Emphasis and the Lack Thereof in Biblical Hebrew." *Maarav* 19 (2012) 181–95.
———. *The Text in the Middle*. New York: Peter Lang, 2014.
———. *The Textual World of the Bible*. New York: Peter Lang, 2013.
———. *The Twelve Prophets in the New Testament*. New York: Peter Lang, 2011.
———. *The Verbal System of Biblical Aramaic: A Distributional Approach*. New York: Peter Lang, 2008.
Smith, H. P. *A Critical and Exegetical Commentary on the Books of Samuel*. International Critical Commentary. Edinburgh: T & T Clark, 1899.
Spellman, Ched. *Toward a Canon-Conscious Reading of the Bible: Exploring the History and Hermeneutics of the Canon*. Sheffield, ENG: Phoenix, 2014.

Bibliography

Sperber, Alexander. *A Historical Grammar of Biblical Hebrew*. Leiden, NLD: Brill, 1966.

Steck, Odil Hannes. *Old Testament Exegesis: A Guide to the Methodology*. Translated by James D. Nogalski. Atlanta: Scholars, 1998.

Sternberg, Meir. *The Poetics of Biblical Narrative: Ideological Literature and the Drama of Reading*. Bloomington, IN: Indiana University Press, 1985.

Steuernagel, Carl. *Lehrbuch der Einleitung in das Alte Testament*. Tübingen: J.C.B. Mohr, 1912.

Stoebe, H. J. "Die Goliathperikope 1 Sam. XVII.1—XVIII.5 und die Textform der Septuaginta." *Vetus Testamentum* 4 (1954) 397–413.

Talmon, Shemaryahu. *Text and Canon of the Hebrew Bible: Collected Studies*. Winona Lake, IN: Eisenbrauns, 2010.

Thackeray, H. St. J. *The Septuagint and Jewish Worship*. London: British Academy, 1921.

Thenius, O. *Die Bücher Samuels*. Leipzig: Weidmann, 1842.

Tigay, Jeffrey H. *The Evolution of the Gilgamesh Epic*. Philadelphia: University of Pennsylvania Press, 1982. Reprint, Wauconda, IL: Bolchazy-Carducci, 2002.

Toorn, Karel van der. *Scribal Culture and the Making of the Hebrew Bible*. Cambridge: Harvard University Press, 2007.

Tov, Emanuel. *The Greek and Hebrew Bible*. Atlanta: SBL, 2006.

———. "The Septuagint as a Source for the Literary Analysis of Hebrew Scriptures." In *Exploring the Origins of the Bible*, edited by Craig A. Evans and Emanuel Tov, 31–56. Grand Rapids: Baker, 2008.

———. *Textual Criticism of the Hebrew Bible*. 3rd ed. Minneapolis: Fortress, 2012.

Trebolle, Julio, and Pablo Torijano. "The Behavior of the Hebrew Medieval Manuscripts and the Vulgate, Aramaic and Syriac Versions of 1–2 Kings vis-à-vis the Masoretic Text and the Greek Version." In *The Text of the Hebrew Bible: From the Rabbis to the Masoretes*, edited by E. Martín-Contreras and L. Miralles-Maciá, 101–33. Göttingen: Vandenhoeck & Ruprecht, 2014.

Ulrich, Eugene. *The Dead Sea Scrolls and the Origins of the Bible*. Grand Rapids: Eerdmans, 1999.

Walker, N. "Concerning the Function of 't'." *Vetus Testamentum* 5 (1955) 314–15.

Waltke, Bruce K., and Michael O'Connor. *An Introduction to Biblical Hebrew Syntax*. Winona Lake, IN: Eisenbrauns, 1990.

Weitzman, Michael. "The Interpretive Character of the Syriac Old Testament." In *Hebrew Bible / Old Testament: The History of Its Interpretation*, vol. 1, *From the Beginnings to the Middle Ages*, edited by Magne Sæbo, 587–611. Göttingen: Vandenhoeck & Ruprecht, 1996.

Welch, Adam C. *The Work of the Chronicler: Its Purpose and Its Date*. London: Oxford University Press, 1939.

Bibliography

Wellhausen, J. *Die Composition des Hexateuchs und der historischen Bücher des Alten Testaments*. 3rd ed. Berlin: G. Reimer, 1899.

Westermann, Claus. *Isaiah 40–66*. Translated by D. M. G. Stalker. Philadelphia: Westminster, 1969.

Willi, T. *Die Chronik als Auslegung*. Göttingen: Vandenhoeck & Ruprecht, 1972.

Wilson, A. M. "The Particle את in Hebrew." *Hebraica* 6 (1889–90) 139–50, 212–24.

Woods, F. H. "The Light Shown by the Septuagint Version." In *Studia Biblica* 1, edited by S. R. Driver et al., 21–38. Oxford: Clarendon, 1885.

Würthwein, Ernst. *The Text of the Old Testament*. 2nd ed. Translated by Erroll F. Rhodes. Grand Rapids: Eerdmans, 1995.

Young, I., et al. *The Linguistic Dating of Biblical Texts*. London: Equinox, 2009.

Zetterholm, Karin Hedner. *Jewish Interpretation of the Bible: Ancient and Contemporary*. Minneapolis: Fortress, 2012.

www.ingramcontent.com/pod-product-compliance
Lightning Source LLC
Chambersburg PA
CBHW070928160426
43193CB00011B/1612